NUMBER 37

THE ENGLISH
EXPERIENCE

ITS RECORD IN EARLY PRINTED BOOKS
PUBLISHED IN FACSIMILE

EDWARD DAVIES

THE ART OF WAR
AND
ENGLANDS TRAYNINGS

LONDON 1619

DA CAPO PRESS
THEATRVM ORBIS TERRARVM LTD.
AMSTERDAM 1968 NEW YORK

The publishers acknowledge their gratitude
to the Trustees of the Bodleian Library, Oxford,
for their permission to reproduce
the Library's copy.

S.T.C.No.6326

Collation: $\P^4$,A^1,B-Z^4,Aa-Ff^4

with one folding plate

Published in 1968 by
Theatrum Orbis Terrarum Ltd.,
O.Z. Voorburgwal 85, Amsterdam
&
Da Capo Press
- a division of Plenum Publishing Corporation -
227 West 17th Street, New York. 10011
Library of Congress Catalog Card Number:

68 – 54633

Printed in The Netherlands

THE
ART OF VVAR,
A N D
ENGLANDS
TRAYNINGS;

PLAINELY
Demonſtrating the dutie of a priuate
SOVLDIER; *with the Office of each ſeuerall* Of-
ficer belonging to a Foot-company : and the
Martiall lawes of the field.

AS ALSO,

The office and charge belonging to the com-
mand of a *Colonell*; the Exerciſe of trayning or
drilling : With diuers other neceſſary and profitable diſciplined NOTES and
Obſeruations.

BY EDW. DAVIES *Gentleman.*

LONDON
Printed by EDWARD GRIFFIN, dwelling in the
Little-Olde-Baily neere the ſigne of the
Kings-head. 1 6 1 9.

TO THE HIGH
AND MIGHTY CHARLES,
ONELY SONNE OF HIS MAIESTY,
Prince of WALES, Duke of CORNEWALL,
YORKE, ALBANIE, and ROTHSAY, Marquiſe of
ORMONT, Earle of CHESTER and ROSS,
Lord of ADMANOCH, and Knight of
the moſt noble Order of the
GARTER.

HE ample and deſerued com-
mendation (which Fame hath
blazed ouer all this Kingdom,
and more and more ſhall to
your eternall memory) of the
ardent zeale that your Highneſſe hath vnto Military Diſcipline, and
the vertuouſly diſpoſed, and of your en-
couragement of them, hath amongſt many
hearts truely deuoted to your Highneſſe in all

ſub-

ſubmiſſiue humilitie, incenſed and animated mine(though moſt vnworthy) to preſent, offer, and dedicate vnto your Highneſſe, this rude, and vnpoliſhed Pamphlet, treating and de-monſtrating the path-way to the youths, and the many vnexpert traine-men of this King-dome, to lead them to the marke, which is to become perfit and abſolute Souldiers. Who (hauing reaped a large harueſt of peace vnder the moſt peacefull Monarch in Europe, your moſt renowmed Father) are very raw and al-together ignorant in moſt points of Militarie Exerciſe. My long continuance in the warres hath by experience gathered, that it is very ne-ceſſarie and requiſite, in the Summer of Peace, to forecaſt and prouide againſt the Winter of Warres. *Mars* hath long time ſlumbered, and as *Ioſua* commanded the Sunne to ſtand firme, ſo our Royall *Ioſua*, our Soueraigne King I A M E s (whom God protect from outward and domeſticall inuaſions) with his glorious beames appearing and entring the Confines of this Kingdome hath diſperſed the clouds, as well of forreine, as home-bred broyles and diſſentions, and eſtabliſhed our peace like Mount Sion: Yet tho *Mars* be fettered, I hold

it

it (vnder your Highneſſe correction) both
conuenient, and agreable with the policie of
other Nations, that this Common-weale be
euer in a readineſſe to preuent accidentall, and
enſuing dangers, leaſt (wallowing too long in
the cradle of Securitie, and *Mars* on a ſuddaine
awaking, and ſounding in our eares vnexpected
Alarmes) it buy Repentance at too deare a rate.
And to regiſter the ſame in the Tablets of my
Country-mens hearts, and for their good, I
haue compiled and collected the obſeruations
and directions in this Booke following; the
which I humbly deſire may be reſpected by
your Highneſſe, not according to the merit of
the action, or matter it ſelfe, but according to
the intent and affection of the Agent and De-
dicator; and that your Highneſſe will imitate
herein that great Patron and Patterne of humilitie, who made more account of the poore widowes mite, than of the ſuperfluitie and abun-
dant treaſure of the rich. And thus with my
vnceſſant prayers to the Almighty, the Lord of
Hoſtes, that your Highneſſe may daily more
and more grow in the fauour of God and Men,
and in the practiſe of all vertuous, pious, and
valorous actions, to the aduancement of Reli-

¶ 3　　　　　　　　gion,

gion, the vanquiſhing of your enemies, and the good of this Common-wealth; crauing pardon for my boldneſs, I humbly take my leaue, and euer reſt with my beſt endeuors,

At your Highneſſe ſeruice

and commandment,

Edward Dauies.

To the READER.

THe exercise of training hath beene much neg-
lected, and chiefly in the Marches of Wales,
till now of late that it hath pleased God, and
the Kings grace, to send vs that thrice worthy Earle of North-hampton, Lord Presi-
dent, established in the principality of his Maiesties Councell in the Marches of Wales &c. For it hath
pleased his Excellencie in times conuenient to call together the
Traine-men; and his Lordship was honourably, and dutifully entertained, and conueied from Shire to Shire by his Lord-
ships Lieutenants of the Shire; and also all the Knights and
best Gentlemen in the Countrey. The Military men being assembled together, it pleased his Lordship to take great paines
in ordering, directing, and exercising both Horse and Foote
most brauely to behold; and his Lordshippe taking speciall
view both of Horse and Foote, where his Lordship apprehen-
ding debilitie and error to be committed amongst them, his
Lordship giueth the Captaines a streight charge, by no meanes,
not to neglect their exercise of training vnder paine, &c.

Likewise, to make it more apparant to the view of the world
of his Lo: affection towards the exercise of Marciall discipline, his Lo: hath now of late called together, not only his Lo:
owne Gentlemen, but also all the Clarkes belonging to the
Councell in the Marches of Wales; and his Lordship being
well prouided of an able Leader, which is one of his Lo: Gentlemen, who in times conuenient doth exercise the said Company.

Moreouer,

To the Reader.

Moreouer, I ought not to omit to relate his Honours due commendations, as also his speciall care of the KINGS Maiesties seruice, to maintaine not onely all Martiall discipline, but also to lead his Ho: Successors to the marke of an honourable subiect; and to performe the same his Lordship is alwaies prouided of 18. goodly and braue young Horses, the which are daily trained in all points of warre (at Luddlow Castle-yard) by one of his Gent: of the Horse, who is an expert and sufficient Rider, &c.

Also it is my part to say somewhat herein of the worthy Rulers, and Gouernours of the Low-countries the schoole of Warre; his Excellencie Graue Mauris hath inuented and set out diuers Postures belonging to the orders both of Pike and Musket, very necessary and profitable for the exercise of armes, the which are maintained and practised by the thrice worthy Commanders, Coronell Cissell, and Coronell Veare; and is directly followed by all other valiant Leaders : the which Postures and Orders are practised in the Artillery-yard, and also in the Military-yard, by worthy Captaines, well experienced in the Martiall discipline, and also they are well prouided of sufficient Officers.

There came a little Pamphlet to my hands wherin I found, and made vse of certaine Orders of the exercising Muskettieres : The said booke was dedicated vnto that worthy Commander Coronell CISSELL, who did much practise the said Orders : *Viz.* also that the said volume was set out by that worthy Leader Captaine WAIMOVTH, who is worthy of great commendations, for his good worke.

The

The Contents of the first Booke.

The Contents of the ſecond Booke.

A ·   *The*

The Contents.

The Contents of the third Booke.

THE

THE
FIRST BOOKE
OF MILITARY
Directions:

In the which is set out how a good Souldier DISNIER and CORPORALL, ought to behaue themselues in *Warres* : Together with the Martiall lawes of the *Field* ; And other necessary *Notes* and *Offices*.

CHAP. I.

And first what is to be required, and necessarie to be observed in a priuate SOVLDIER.

HE plat-forme of a Fortresse , by how much more it is planted vpon a sure foundation , by so much more it is participant of a firme and forcible perfection : which reason duly considered it ought to lead euery man so to rule himselfe in all his affaires, as he may be both apt to receiue, and able to performe all vertuous and valorous actions. Therefor he

B   that

that defires to become a Souldier of affured good qualitie, to the intent he may be able to perfeuer in each enterprife, beare out euery brunt ftoutly, and ferue fufficiently, he ought to haue a ftrong body, found, free from
ficknefle, and of a good complexion : So fhall he be able
to refift the continuall toile and trauell, which of necefli-
tie he muft daily take, as continuall and extreame cold in
the winter, immoderate heate in the fummer, in marching in the day, keeping fentinell in the night, and in his
cold cabben, in fecret ambufhes, and in trenches, where
perchance he fhall ftand a number of houres in the water and mire vp to the knees : and befides vpon bulwarkes, breaches in efpialls, in fentinels, perdues, and
fuch like, when occafion requires and neceffitie conftraines : of all which exploites and difcommodities hee
muft perforce be partaker.

Wherefore that man which is not of fuch fufficiencie
in body (to the end he fpend not his time in vaine) it is
very requifite he refolue himfelfe to exercife fome other
profeffion, for although fome doe hold that few men be
ftrong by nature, but many by exercife and induftrie :
yet that notwithftanding ftrength of body is firft to be
required, in refpeſt that a Souldier muft be afwell acquainted, and as able to beare continuall trauell, as a bird
can endure to flie, yea and to put on a refolute minde, to
beare all the miferies and hazardes of warlike affaires.
A Souldier is generally to be chofen betwixt 18. and
46. yeares.

Moreouer, I fuppofe it moft neceffarie, that euery man
according to the nature of his body, and inclined motion
of his minde, make election of his armes and weapons,
as of pike, halbert, or hargabufe : Neuertheleffe refpeſt
ought

ought to be had to the proportion of his perfon, and to take fuch armes as doth beſt agree with the fame: to a tall man a pike, to a meane ſtature a halberd, and to a little nimble perfon a peece. But if he preferre his proper difpoſition betore the qualitie of his perfon, it is very neceſſarie he exerciſe that weapon he makes choiſe of, to the intent he may attaine vnto a moſt perfect practiſe of the fame, for as no man at the firſt time when he takes any toole or inſtrument in his hand, growes immediately at that inſtant to be a perfect artificer : euen ſo it is with a Souldier, vntill experience hath inſtructed him : touching which I meane to ſay fomewhat.

He which ſeekes to attaine and attribute to himſelfe the honourable name of a Souldier, muſt firſt employ his time in practiſe of thoſe armes wherewith he meanes to ſerue, and ſo apply his time, that when any enterpriſe ſhall call him forth to make proofe thereof, he may be able to handle his peece with due dexterity, and his pike with an aſſured agilitie : ſince thoſe be the weapons wherwith now *Mars* doth moſt commonly arme his warlike troupe, and trie each doubtfull fight of bloudy battaile : for in this our age experience and practiſe makes apparant that Archers amongſt forreine Nations be neuer vſed, and the halberd but either amongſt few or few in number. The Archer ſerues to ſmall purpoſe, but when he is ſhadowed with ſome trench or bulwarke free from hargabuſe or musket-ſhot : Or that lyning a band of Hargabuſiers, hee doth ſecond them in any inuading onſet, and then a whole flight of arrowes, ſo that they be light and able to flie aboue twelueſcore, will maruellouſly gaule any maine battell of footemen or Squadron of Horſemen. The Halberd likewiſe doth onely ſerue in

B 2 the

the ſacke of a towne, in a breach, in a ſally, or canuiſado, to enter a houſe, or in the throng of a ſtroken battell to execute ſlaughter ; wherefore touching theſe two weapons, vnleſſe neceſſitie conſtraine, and that Hargabuſiers be wanting, Archers may well be ſpared : and theſe great numbers of Halberdiers and Bill-men, which are and haue beene in times paſt vſed in *England*, may well be left off, ſaue a few to guard euery Enſigne, and to attend vpon the Colonell, or Captaine, which in an armie will amount to a ſufficient number to depreſſe the ouercome and flying enemy.

Therefore a Souldier muſt either accuſtome himſelfe to beare a peece or Pike : if he beare a peece, then muſt he firſt learne to hold the ſame, to accommodate his match betweene his two formoſt fingers and his thombe, and to plant the great end on his breaſt with a gallant Souldier-like grace : and being ignorant, to the intent he may bee more encouraged, let him acquaint himſelfe firſt with the firing of touch-pouder in his panne, and ſo by degrees both to ſhoote off, to bow and beare vp his body, and ſo conſequently to attaine to the leuell and practiſe of an aſſured and ſeruiceable ſhot, readily charge, and with a comely couch diſcharge, making choiſe at the ſame inſtant of his marke with a quicke and vigilant eie.

His flaſke and touch-box muſt keepe his pouder, his purſe and mouth his bullets : in skirmiſh his left hand muſt hold his match and peece, and the right hand vſe the office of charging and diſcharging.

Being againſt the enemie, whilſt with an indented courſe he doth trauell his plaine ground, or elſe takes aduantage of his place and inuaſion, as vnder the ſafegard of a trench, the backe of a ditch, old-wall, tree or ſuch
like :

like : let him euer firſt load his peece with pouder out of
his flaske, then with her bullet, and laſt with amuring,
and touch-pouder, foreſeeing euer that the panne bee
cleane, the couer cloſe, and the tutch-hole wide, or elſe
well proind : ſo that ſtill obſeruing modeſt order in his
trauerſe, neither ouerflow, nor ouer-ſpeedy, to the en-
tent he become not each mans marke through his ſlug-
giſhneſſe, nor runne himſelfe out of breath through his
owne raſhneſſe, for the moſt part keeping his ſide towards his enemie : let him diſcharge going, but neuer
ſtanding : ſo ſhall he the better ſhunne the enemies ſhot
and chuſe his aſſured aduantage.

A ſouldier ought to be carefull that his furniture bee
good, ſubſtantiall and ſtaunch from raine, the charge of
his flaske iuſt for his peece, and the ſpring quicke and
ſharpe : The pipe of his touch-box ſomewhat wide, that
the pouder may haue free paſſage, which otherwiſe
would choake vp.

In time of marching, and trauelling by the way let
him keepe a paper in the panne and tutch-hole, and in
wet weather haue a caſe for his peece ſomewhat portable,
or elſe of neceſſitie he muſt keepe the ſame from wet vnder his arme-hole or caſſocke, or by ſome other inuention free from damage of the weather, and his match in his
pocket, onely that except which he burnes : and that likewiſe ſo cloſe in the hollow of his hand, or ſome artificiall
pipe of pewter hanging at his girdle, as the coale by wet
or water go not out.

It is moreouer requiſite, that a ſouldier keepe his cocke
with oyle free in falling, and his peece bright without
ruſting, neither muſt he want his neceſſarie tooles, as a
ſcowrer, tirebale and worme, hauing euery one a vice to

turne

turne into the end of the ſcouring ſticke, ſo that if through
wet weather or any other accident, his peece will not be
diſcharged, the skilfull Souldier may with his tireball pull
out his bullet, with the worme, the paper and wet pouder, and with his ſcourer make his peece cleane within:
His ſcourer muſt be trimmed on the end with a linnen-
cloth of a ſufficient ſubſtance, therewith to make cleane
the cannon of his peece within. The one end of his ſcouring ſticke ought to haue a round end of bone of iuſt big-
neſſe with the mouth of his peece, therewithall at his
pleaſure to ramme in pouder and paper, or in ſteed of paper, ſuch ſoft haire as they ſtuffe ſaddles withall, the danger whereof is not like : but this the Souldier muſt vſe
when time permits. During the time of his ſeruice let
him euer haue a diligent care to keepe his peece cleane
and bright within, and once a fortnight, or at the leaſt
once a month take out the breech and throroughly view
and waſh the barrell within, to ſee whether it hath any
flawes, brackes, chambers, frettings, or ruptures, which
would endanger the breaking thereof, eſpecially if before
hand the end of his bare ſcourer haue giuen him any
cauſe to ſuſpect ſuch faults, to the intent he may change
the ſame for a new for feare of ſpoiling himſelfe.

He that loues the ſaftie of his owne perſon, and de-
lights in the goodneſſe and beauty of a peece, let him alwaies make choiſe of one that is double breeched, and if
it be poſſible a myllan peece, for they be of a tough and
perfect temper, light, ſquare, and bigge of breech, and
very ſtrong where the pouder doth lie, and where the violent force of the fire doth conſiſt, and notwithſtanding
thinne at the end.

Our Engliſh peeces approach very neere vnto them
                                                    in

in goodneſſe and beautie (their heauineſſe only excepted) ſo that they be made of purpoſe, and not one of
theſe common ſale peeces with round barrells, whereunto a beaten ſouldier will haue great reſpect, and chooſe
rather to pay double money for a good peece, then to
ſpare his purſe and endanger himſelfe.

But to returne to my matter, let a ſouldier haue hanging euer at the ſtrings of his tutch-box, or ſome other readie part of his garment, a couple of proyning pinnes at
the leaſt, that if by fortune the tutch-hole of his peece be
ſtopped or furred vp, hee may therewith both make his
pan cleane, and yeeld a ready paſſage that the fire may
haue her courſe, by incorporating both the tutch-pouder
without, and the corne-pouder within together. But a
ready Souldier will alwaies fore-ſee that the tutch hole
be ſo wide, as the pouder without in the pan may haue
free concourſe to that within the peece, thereby to haſten
more ſpeedy diſcharge, conſidering a ſouldier cannot
haue leaſure and commoditie to proine his peece at all
times, but muſt of neceſſitie vſe a great dexterity.

But ſince I am falne into the ſpeech of a quicke charge,
and nimble diſcharge, I will by the way declare the opinion of certaine nations therein.

Experience of late daies hath taught vs, that thoſe
Nations which follow the warres, inuent euery way how
they may endomage the enemie in all their enterpriſes,
but eſpecially in skirmiſh, which for the moſt part conſiſts in ſhot, and by ſuch as can with the eye of his minde
make an aſſured leuell, and with a nimble diſcharge, both
chooſe out and kill his enemie.

And therefore thoſe ſouldiers which in our time haue
beene for the moſt part leuied in the Low-countries,
                                                    eſpecially

especially, those of *Artoyes* and *Henault*, called by the generall name of *Wallownes* haue vfed to hang about their neckes, vpon a baudricke or border, or at their girdles certaine pipes which they call charges, of copper and tin made with couers, which they thinke in skirmifh to bee the moft readie way. But the *Spaniard* difpifing that order, doth altogether vfe his flaske.

The *French-man*, both charge and flaske. But fome of our *Englifh-nation*, their pocket, which in refpect of the danger of the fparkes of their match, the vncertaine charge, the expence and fpoile of pouder, the difcommoditie of wet, I account more apt for the fhow of a triumph and wanton skirmifh before Ladies and Gentlewomen, then fit for the field, in a day of feruice in the face of the enemy: and in like fort the charge which either doth fhed and loofe his pouder whilft a Souldier doth trauerfe his ground, or elfe is fo cloddered and rammed together, that he fhall be forced fometimes to faile of halfe his charge. Therefore I conclude with the *Spaniard*, that a good flaske is that which is moft warlike and ready in feruice without the curious helpe of any extraordinary inuention.

One of the greateft helpes confifts in pouder and match: for a Souldier muft euer buy his pouder fharpe in tafte, well incorporate with falt-peter, and not full of coole-duft. Let him accuftome to drie his pouder if hee can in the funne, firft fprinkled ouer with *Aqua-vitæ* or ftrong Claret-wine &c. Let him make his tutch-pouder, being finely farfed and fifted, with quick-pale, which is to be bought at the Pouder-makers or Apothecaries: and let his match be fo boiled in afhes, lye and pouder, that it will both burne well, carrie a long coale, and that will

not

not breake off with the touch of your finger. The preparations will at the firft touch giue fire, and procure a violent, fpeedy, and thundering difcharge. Some vfe brimftone finely poudered in their tutch-pouder, but that furs and ftops vp your breech and tutch-hole.

The bullet of a fouldiers peece muft be of a iuft bigneffe with the mouth of the fame, fo that falling in fmoothly, it may driue downe, and clofe vp the mouth of the pouder. Some contrary to the lawes of the field vfe chaine-fhot, and quarter-fhot, which is good in the defence of a breach, to keepe a fortreffe, or vpon fhipboard: but being daily vfed, it will gaule a peece within, and put it in hazard to breake, fpecially in a long skirmifh when the barrell is hot.

Note that after his peece is very hoate, let the Souldier if he can, giue fomewhat a leffe charge for feare of burfting his peece, vnleffe he haue good triall thereof. If the ftocke of his peece be crooked, he ought to place the end iuft before aboue his left pappe: if long and ftraight, as the *Spaniards* vfe them, then vpon the point of his right fhoulder, vfing a ftately vpright pace in difcharge.

It is not in vaine to aduertife him, that in skirmifh hee muft hold his peece betwixt his thombe and the ends of his fingers, which I account a fure meane, betwixt griping of the barrell, and laying the fame onely vpon his foremoft finger and thombe, for the one is ouer dangerous, and the other altogether vnfteedy.

I iudge it likewife moft conuenient for him, to take hold of his peece with his left hand in that part of the wood (wherein the barrell lies) there as the peece is of moft equall ballance. Although fome accuftome themfelues to hold it iuft vnder the cocke, by reafon whereof

C   he

he ſhall be enforced to change his hand if he charge out of a flaske, into the midſt of the peece, to bring downe the mouth to his flaske which is great delay and hinderance in skirmiſh. So to conclude, he that meanes to be accompted a forward and perfect good ſhot, by continuall exerciſe muſt be ſo ready, that in all particular points touching his peece, pouder, match, bullets, and the vſe of them, that he neither be to ſeeke, nor grow amazed in the furious rage of *Bellonas* fiery skirmiſhes, her ſuddaine ſurpriſes, and bloody ſlaughter of dangerous aſſaults of cruell battailes.

The Musket is to be vſed in all reſpects like vnto the Hargabuſe, ſaue that in reſpect he carries a double bullet, and is much more weightie. He vſeth a ſtaffe breaſt-high, in the one end a pike to pitch in the ground, and in the other an iron forke to reſt his peece vpon, and a hoale a little beneath the ſame in the ſtaffe: whereunto he doth adde a ſtring, which tied and wrapped about his wreſt, yeelds him commodity to traine his forke or ſtaffe after him whilſt he in skirmiſh doth charge his Musket afreſh with pouder and bullet.

Now to ſpeake ſomewhat of a Pike-mans charge, a few words ſhall ſuffice, becauſe I will not be ouer-tedious. Let him learne to toſſe his pike, couch and croſſe the ſame, to receiue the violent charge of Horſe-men, to front the furious ſhocke of foote-men, and be able to furniſh out his fight both a farre off and neere hand: Which Notes with the like will be ſufficient, by reaſon that he is for the moſt part put to ſtand in a maine and ſquare-battaile. Both the Hargabuſier and Pike-man muſt weare a ſhort rapier and a ſmall poinado: for if in the middeſt of Encounters and Skirmiſhes, they be driuen

uen to vſe them, their length is an occaſion they cannot
be drawne, vnleſſe he abandon his peece or pike, whereby he ſhall either looſe his pike, or want his rapier, which
at the Sera and cloſe is very neceſſarie both for defence
and offence : contrary to the careleſſe cuſtome of ſome,
whom I haue ſeene come into the field without rapier or
dagger, which was an aſſured argument, that their heeles
ſhould be their target, and their ſhamefull flight their
ſafety, when their pouder was ſpent.

Now as theſe careleſſe perſons farre miſſe the marke
with ouer great ſecuritie, ſo ſome bring in a cuſtome of
too much curioſitie in arming Hargabuſiers, for beſides
a peece, flaske, tutch-box, rapier and dagger : they loade
them with a heauie ſhirt of male, and a Burganet : ſo that
by that time they haue marched in the heat of the ſom-
mer or deepe of the winter ten or twelue Engliſh-miles,
they are more apt to reſt, then ready to fight, whereby it
comes to paſſe that either the enterpriſe they go about,
which requires celerity, ſhall become fruſtrate by reaſon
of the ſtay they make in refreſhing themſelues, or elſe
they are in danger to be repulſed for want of luſtineſſe,
breath, and agilitie.

Wherefore in mine opinion it is not neceſſarie, that
this extraordinarie arming of ſhot ſhould be vſed, but in
ſurpriſes of Townes, Eſcalades, and aſſaults of breaches,
to defend the Souldiers heads from ſtones, and ſuch ſtuffe
as they beſieged haue prepared to driue them from their
enterpriſe: Or elſe in ſome ſpeciall ſet battaile againſt the
cut and thruſt of weapons: which exploits, for that they
be not ſo ordinary as is the skirmiſh, ſo are theſe armes
nothing ſo neceſſarie, but rather a burthen more beautifull then beneficiall, and of greater charge then commo-

C 2   ditie;

ditie; ſpecially a ſhirt of male, which is very dangerous, for ſhot, if a number of thoſe ſmall peeces ſhould bee driuen into a mans body by a bullet.

The furniture due to a Pike-man beſides his pike, rapier and dagger, conſiſting of a common corſelet, hauing a coller, curiat, taſes, back-part, poldrowes, wambraſſes, and burganets for the head, for that they be ſufficiently knowne, becauſe I will not be ouer prolixe vpon euery particular point, I will onely ſay thus much more touching the Pike-man, that he ought to haue his pike at the point and middeſt trimmed with handſome taſſels, and a handle, not ſo much for ornament as to defend the Souldiers body from water, which in raine doth runne downe alongſt the wood.

Euery Souldier ought to carry his Hargabuſe, Pike or Halberd, vpon that ſhoulder and ſide, which is outward in ranke, for that ſide which is diſcouered inward is more defended by the generall order that is kept, then any of the other. Which order of carrying armes, is not onely ready and commodious to vſe at all occaſions, but alſo doth make a gallant ſhew, and a generall forme of good proportion, and true proſpect: a thing moſt neceſſarie for a man of valour to vſe in all his doings.

He ought likewiſe euer to haue good regard to weare his weapon of like length the other Souldiers vſe, which in marching doth make the rankes to be of one iuſt line, and in ſhew of a ſeemely and ſtreight proportion, cauſing the whole band to carry a braue and ſingular grace.

A Souldier ought euer to retaine and keepe his armes in ſaftie and forth comming, for he is more to be deteſted then a Coward, that will looſe or play away any part thereof, or refuſe it for his eaſe, or to auoide paines:

Where-

Wherefore fuch a one is to be difmiffed with punifhment, or made fome abiect Pioner. Therefore during
his feruice and after his returne home, let him ftill bee
wedded to his weapons and armour, that when he is called vpon againe to ferue his Prince, he be not enforced to
furnifh himfelfe againe with new Armes, fometimes
old, of little value, and leffe goodneffe: as fome fouldiers
now adaies to their great difcommendation doe vfe. A
cuftome altogether different from the true exercife of
armes, and varying from the rule of other warlike-nati-
ons, which make true profeffion of armes : amongft the
which the *Spaniards* and *Zuitʒers* at this day are to bee
commended ; the one for obferuing an apt, fumptuous,
and warlike choife therein, and the other for that they
beare all forts of armes with great aduantage, both in
length and ftrength, the which vnto them becomes very
familiar through the abilitie of body they poffeffe.

Thofe Souldiers which cannot endure the toile and
trauell to beare armes of defence, namely the Pikeman
and Halberdier are made fubiect to receiue both blowes
and death by the hands of their enemies, or through
their difaduantage to take a fhamefull flight, or at the firft
encounter to remaine their prifoners.

Therefore it is very neceffarie for a Souldier to take
paines in daily practife, & to acquaint himfelfe throughly in the exercife and carriage of armes, whereof hee
ought to vfe practife, fpecially of thofe that be offenfiue,
and in thofe which ordinarily we are accuftomed to carrie, as the Rapier, and Dagger, Pike, and Halberd and
fuch like, without making open and apparent profeffion
of the practife thereof, but fecret and feuerall from the
wide fight of the world, that afterwards he may put the

C 3   fame

fame in practife to his greater aduantage and commendation.

Finally the Halberdier, who is armed either with brigandine or corflet, ought of duty to attend with his halberd when his turne comes about his Enfigne, in marching, and fet fquares, in the Captaines lodging and tent for his guard, and at the entrance of a houfe &c. to be the foremoft perfon to force the paffage.

But in a day of battaile the old *Romane* fhield and a fhort fharpe-pointed fword, to execute in a throng of men, exceedes the Halberd and browne-bill.

Befides the Pikeman which is armed all ouer with a corflet, and is to performe his duty in a maine fquare, ftand, or battaile, to receiue the fhocke of horfemen, or charge of the enemies infantery;

There be yet another fort of light-armed Pikes, which onely haue the fore-part of a corflet, and a head-peece, as is the *Almaine* riuet, or good light-iacke, or plate-coate: thefe fometimes may be fent amongft the forlorne-hope of Hargabufiers, to defend them from the inuafions of Horfe-men.

But touching fhot, I would wifh our Nation, being men of ftrong conftitution of body, to beare a Peece betwixt the boare of a Caliuer and a Musket, the which with fmall vfe they would be able to weeld very well at the armes end; which would cary a great aduantage in skirmifh: the which like vnto the Hargabufe, they might (as I faid before) exercife, and with a gallant and affured raifing-vp the crooked end of the ftocke, to his breaft, hauing before hand fitted the coale of his match to giue quicke and iuft fire, whereof euer he muft take the certaine meafure, muft then difcharge amidft his modeft

deft trauerfe, to his greateft aduantage, and to endomage his enemies: Which done he muft firft fold-vp againe the falne march in a ready and conuenient fort betwixt his fingers, hauing both the ends of his match light at once, that whilft the one is fpent, and in kindling againe, the other may ferue his turne.

Befides thefe forefaid weapons I would not thinke it inconuenient, to haue in a Band certain targets of proofe to march in the front, which were very neceffarie to defend a ranke of men in a ftreight-lane, paffage, breach or other place from the enemies fhot, they all clofely and in a low order marching vnder the fauour and fhade of them: as in a skirmifh I faw put in practife, when *Caſſimire* did march with the S T A T E S armie vnder *Louaine*, 1578.

The Captaine is to fet downe by the Generals appointment, the fumme of all their paies, and the difference therein, according to euery mans weapon and qualitie. But to fpeake of other directions and militarie obferuations;

A foot-man that is a Souldier, ought aboue all things to be obedient to his Captaine and officers, and neuer abandon his Enfigne, nor be abfent from his companie without leaue or fpeciall let. In his march hee ought to be modeft, ready in his ranke, obferue a long diftance in his Laumband, and keepe an equall ftay in his Alta.

If words of aduertifement doe paffe ouer from ranke to ranke alongft the marching band, let him deliuer thofe words plainely and with diligence, which the Captaine giues ouer to be pronounced from mouth to mouth, as to paffe Parole appertaines.

If the enemie caufe fodaine Arme, let his bale en bouche and

and his match in the cocke ſhew his ready good-will either to receiue repulſe, or giue charge.

If either for pleaſure in a muſter, or in any other ſhew in ſport or earneſt, his Company be commanded to diſcharge certaine volies of ſhot, or a Salua, he muſt either hold his peece ſidelong the rankes, whilſt he doth prepare the ſame, or with the end higher then their heades, and diſcharge ouer the toppes of the formoſt rankes, for feare of hurting his Companions : which rule they ought to obſerue, and thereunto be conſtrained, vpon paine of ſeuere puniſhment.

If any enterpriſe be made in the night, let him not only keepe his match cloſe from open ſhew, or falling ſparkes, but be vigilant and keepe ſilence, to the intent that through his negligence and noiſe their actions be not diſcouered.

If he keepe Sentinell, and haue the watch-word, let him giue eare diligently to all rumours, noiſes, and view warily all ſuſpected places, to the intent if he heare any trampling, neying of horſes, or approaching enemie (which he may the more eaſily heare by making a hole in the ground, and laying his eare to the ſame) or that he doth ſee the twinkling light of matches, or perceiue any other preſumption of the enemie, hee may either by diſcharging his peece, and crying Saint *George*, arme, arme, giue warning to the next Corpes of guard, that the enemie doth approach, or elſe if his ſuddaine inuaſion require not preſent aduertiſement, he may deferre the report thereof vntill the comming of the next round, vnto whom he muſt from point to point declare what he hath ſeene and heard.

During the time of his Sentinell, hee ought to keepe
himſelfe

himfelfe very clofe, wakefull, fecret, and without noife or rumour, his match clofe and fure from feeing, and his peece ready charged, loaden with her bullet, and proind with tutch-pouder.

If the Round or any other Officer come to fearch to watch and Sentinels, when he doth firft heare or fee them approach, let him fo foone as he doth perceiue them, demaund with a loud voice, *Qui va la ?* Who goes there? to which when anfwere is made, Friends, and that they draw neerer, then let him call to them and commaund that all the whole troupe, but onely one with the watchword, to make prefent ftay, vntill the word be giuen. And if at the fame inftant another Round fhould come another way, let him caufe the one of them to paufe and abide ftill, vntill he haue receiued the word of the other, that thereby he may auoide the inuironing fnares of forraine or priuie enemies, which might by that meanes furprife him.

Therefore in this refpect let him take great care, efpecially before a Towne befieged, or about the circuit of a Campe, and that he alwaies remember to receiue him that giues the word at the end of his peece or pike, and out of danger, hauing his match ready in his Cocke, ready to giue fire, thereby to reward him with a bullet as an enemie, if he giue a wrong word, or entertaine him as a friend if he giue the right : for vnder colour of giuing the word, many Sentinels haue loft their liues, and fuddaine furprifes and canuifados haue beene giuen.

If in the night Arme be giuen in the Campe, he muft make repaire immediately with his peece and furniture to his Enfigne, where he fhall be employed as occafion doth offer.

D   That

That he may be the more ready at any ſuddaine Arme, lying in a towne in Garriſon, and being furried and lodged in a houſe, he ought to haue all the night burning in his chamber by him a candle or lampe, or at the leaſt his fire ſo well raked vp as he may light a candle at the coales with a match of brimſtone, or otherwiſe : that thereby hee may the more ſpeedily not onely finde his armes (which of purpoſe he ought to lay readily in an ordinarie place) but alſo be better able to prepare himſelfe, and kindle his match with all ſpeede.

Note that a Souldier in Garriſon being furried in a houſe, is allowed the beſt bed and chamber ſaue one, faire ſheetes, board-clothes, plates, napkins, towels, dreſſing of his meate, ſeruice at the table, oile, vineger, ſalt, muſtard, candle-light, fire, &c.

Whileſt a Souldier is in the Campe, he ought neuer to lie out-of his clothes, his peece ready charged muſt lye by his ſide, his furniture at his girdle, which is his flaſke, match and tutch-boxe, his rapier very ready, and his poinado likewiſe at his girdle, which if they ſhould be ſo monſtrous daggers, or ſuch a Cutlers ſhoppe as our Engliſh Fencers are accuſtomed to weare, they would be both combrous in cariage, and troubleſome to his Companions, and to himſelfe, eſpecially when they lye in their Cabbins.

A Souldier in Campe muſt make choiſe of two or three or more Camerades, ſuch as for experience, fidelitie, and conditions, doe beſt agree with his nature, that be tied Souldiers and truſtie friends, to the intent that like louing brethren, they may ſupport one another in all aduerſe fortune, and ſupply each others wants. As for example, hauing marched all day, and comming at night

to

to the place where they muſt encampe, one of them
chooſeth out the drieſt and warmeſt plot of ground he
can get in the quarter, which is appointed to his band for
lodging place, doth keepe all their Clokes, Armes, and
Baggage, whileſt another makes prouiſion with one of
their boies, in ſome adioyning village (if time and ſafety
from the enemie doth permit) for long ſtraw, both to
couer their cabbin, and make their bed of : during the
time that an other with a little hatchet (which with a le-
ther bottle for drinke, a little kettle to ſeeth meate in, and
a bagge of ſalt, which are to be borne of the boyes a-
mongſt other Baggage, and are moſt neceſſarie things for
encamping) doth cut downe forked bowes and long
poales to frame and reare vp their cabbin withall, and
prouide timber, or firewood, if it be in winter, or when
need requires, whilſt another doth viſite vniandiers and
victualers (if any follow the campe) for bread, drinke,
and other cates, if otherwiſe they be not prouided by
forrage or picoree, and makes a hole in the earth, wherein hauing made a fire, ſtroken two forked ſtakes at either
ſide, and hanged his kettle to ſeath vpon a cudgell of
wood vpon the ſame, or that for roſt meate hee makes a
ſpit, wodden gauberds, &c. And whilſt thus euery one
is occupied about their neceſſarie occaſions at one inſtant,
they may in due time make prouiſion for all their wants,
and by meanes of this league of amitie amongſt them,
enioy a ſufficient time to reſt their wearied bodies, which
otherwiſe would be hard to be done.

  Therefore I iudge it very requiſite that the whole number vnder the charge of a Deſnier or cheife of a chamber,
ſhould linke themſelues together in perfect friendſhippe,
and aſwell in skirmiſh and fight aide one another, as in all

other

other actions, by which inuincible knot they should receiue wonderfull commoditie.

It imports much that a Souldier should be tractable, for a man cannot imagine a thing either more ingenuous or better, then due and conuenient ciuility. Therefore let him accustome himselfe rather to be of a Saturnine and feuere condition then a common Skoffer, and an ordinarie make-sport, that he may continue in friendship with his companions, and continually remaine in their amitie.

Moreouer, he is much to be commended, which aptly with facilitie and great dexterity can be conuersant with euery one : wherein if a man doe not with great iudgement very circumspectly gouerne himselfe, hee shall for the most part incurre the euill will of those in whose companie hee remaines. The which dealing is of great importance, aswell for the interest of his life, and proper honour and credite, by which meanes the one and the other doth hang in ballance, as also for that he cannot, being drawne away with debates, apply himselfe diligently to follow the warres and seruice of his Captaine : the which ought to be his chiefest obiect and end. For discord amongst men of this Honourable profession, doth hasten, and occasion very much the destruction of their well doing ; and altogether hinder whatsoeuer they take in hand, by reason of the suspicions, discordes, despite, and other respects which of necessitie are commonly accustomed to grow and ensue.

Besides, he must be so moderate in spending his wages, that he be not constrained before the midst of his pay, either to follow the spoile, or borrow of others : whereof springeth a naughtie reputation and a great discredit : yet

not-

notwithstanding he must not suffer himselfe to be noted for a couetous person, or as some say, the enemie of himselfe : that is, by sparing nigardly, to finde a great want and extremitie in necessarie things appertaining to his apparell and victuals, whose expences ought cheifly to be in galant Armor and furniture.

Note that the pay and wages which he receiues of his Captaine and Treasurer, must not be taken or thought to serue or supply for any other vse , but to sustaine life with victuals, keepe him apparelled, and maintaine his armes. Therefore ought it to be gouerned discreetly and orderly at all times, in what place soeuer he shall remaine, either in the campe, ciuill cities, or in his proper house, as well to keepe himselfe in health, as cheifly to make apparant to his Captaine the noble motion of his minde : So that pricked forward by this spurre of honour, and not for any other extraordinarie and base occasion, a good souldier is continually constrained to win credite, despising all other dealing which ariseth from hope of commodity and greedy gaine, the way to make a man esteemed to carrie a base minde, and almost not disagreeing from brute breasts without reason. For these priuate Souldiers which seeke by such meanes as be extraordinarie, to aduance themselues aboue their proper pay, without doubt giue an euill presage of themselues, and so euill that it should be better for them to apply their time in some other sort, as about merchandise and other occupations, rather then follow the honourable exercise of Armes, which is altogether grounded vpon a noble minde, valiant courage, and extreame trauell of body.

He must dispose himselfe to be very diligent in what exercise or enterprise soeuer he shall be put vnto, as to

make

make Sentinell : wherein it is conuenient, as I haue touched before, that he be very vigilant when it is his lot to be commanded thereunto, that in doing the contrarie, there ſucceed not a moſt rigorous chaſtiſement by leauing his body dead behind him, as it may very well fall out, and to whom it may be ſaid, I left him as I found him, ſince ſleepe is the image of death.

A good Souldier ought continually to accompany the Enſigne, and haue ſpeciall regard, that the ſame fall not in danger of ſurpriſing by the enemie, and that he endeauour himſelfe by all meanes without any reſpect of danger to preſerue and recouer the ſame : for the loſſe thereof is a perpetuall ſhame to the whole band. And therefore he ought at no time to abandon the ſame for any occaſion, but lodge himſelfe ſo neere it as he can, to the intent that amongſt the reſt, if it be poſſible, he may be one of the firſt at all rumours of armes, and ſodaine alarums, aſwell by day as night. And being armed with the weapon he caries, hauing conducted his Enſigne to the place appointed, by the head Officers, he may in the ſight of his Captaine (ſhewing a moderate forwardneſſe and deſire) breed an opinion of his courage and valor : ſo that when occaſion doth offer, his Captaine amongſt the reſt may make ſpeciall choiſe of him.

He muſt for no occaſion abſent himſelfe, or go to any far diſtant place about any enterpriſe or booty of picoree, without the expreſſe licence of his Captaine : for he that is once become a Souldier is now no more his own man, but his vnder whoſe gouernment he is paide : who deſiring to ſerue his turne when occaſions be miniſtred in time of warres, not hauing his valiant and beſt Souldiers preſent and ready about him, ſhall not onely be made

fruſtrate

fruftrate of that he would performe, but fometimes alfo
fuffer and fuftaine damage, and onely in refpect of thofe
which be abfent abroad at their owne pleafure, contrary
to the confent and knowledge of the Captaine.

He ought fufficiently to eate, reft and fleepe, whileft
time doth permit, to the end he be not called for vnprouided, and that he may the more readily performe all enterprifes needfull, without any difcommodity or want of
abilitie, which commonly doe fall out vnlooked for, and
vpon the fodaine, for in ordinary and accuftomed enterprifes, it is an eafie thing to finde euery fouldier prouided, but in fodaine furprifes not. Befides, I thinke it appertaines and is proper to a good Souldier, to follow the
warres fo long as he poffibly can, for the increafe of his
experience. But being conftrained to returne into his
Countrey, or into any Citie, fortreffe or other place of
defence, by reafon of fome truce, feconded by peace, or
through any other accident, which doth conftraine him
to abandon the warres : then it is neceffary he fall to exercife that Art, wherein he chiefly hath been brought vp,
either in merchandife, handicraft, or hufbandrie, or elfe
whatfoeuer, thereby to fupply his neceffities, to exercife
his body, and to liue honeftly : and by that meanes flie
idleneffe, a thing moft incident to youth : who being altogether ignorant in treading the fteppes of a ftaied life
(through the fmall experience hee hath of the world,
which by tract of time is obtained, and by long practife,
fpecially in the exercife of armes) perfwades himfelfe he
fhall winne credit and commodity through the meanes
of infolent actions, which altogether ought to be abhor-
red : through rafh and prodigall brauerie, which oftentimes torments innocent Families and poore Parents:
and

and through galant garments and fumptuous attire,
whereby they grow Bankerout: fo that they are brought
in time (being intangled in thofe fweete traps faueft and
fharpe fhowers) to runne headlong into a thoufand and
moft miferable ruines. Therefore good Souldiers ought
fpecially to endeauour themfelues by fome commendable induftrie to gaine the good grace of valorous and valiant Captaines, and mightie Princes, the true Poffeffors
and fathers of warre, through whofe authoritie and commendation they may be preferred : for the faith and affured credit of all warlike and worthy Souldiers doth depend vpon men of valour, and not of weake authoritie,
fmall valor; and great abufe of the ignorant and com-
mon-people, called the beaft with many heades. Therefore let them euer obferue the honor of the good and vertuous : for fince that in time of warres euery fouldier of
good conditions doth fharpen his wit, and willingly aduenture his life, not refpecting toyles or trauell, expences
or danger, but doth imploy his induftrie to preferre his
Princes profite, by great reafon in time of peace he ought
to be aduanced and maintained by them : and much the
more for himfelfe, is to vfe all his indeauour to compaffe
his owne commoditie, and thereby make manifeft his
proper vertue, the which doth not confift in outward appearance of valour and difcretion : but in the true action
thereof, agreeable to his honourable profeffion.

A fouldier muft apparell himfelfe in the warres with
cloth of frefh colour, profitable and commodious : a-
mongft the reft, red, murry, tauny and fcarlet makes a
galant fhew in the field, which he muft weare to honour
the militarie profeffion, and for his moft fit and apt
wearing, and not to hinder the difpofition of his mem-
bers

bers, as doth our great bumbafted and bolſtered hoſe, which not many yeeres ſince hath beene vſed : but in ſteed of them a ſtraite brabantie and gaſcaine is to bee worne, together with a cloſe caſſocke, which may ſhield both his flaske, tutch-box, his match and peece from raine if need be, whereby he may be ready to execute a- ny enterpriſe he is commanded to performe, and that of neceſſitie he ought to doe : and ſo arme himſelfe in other reſpects, that he may readily doe any ſeruice hee is aſ- ſigned vnto.

He muſt be willing to put in prooſe all things comman- ded, without making reply, or denying any one thing, or deferring the matter from one time to another, either for feare of ſpoiling or ſpotting his apparell in foule-way, or foule-weather, or that he ſhall not be able to inioy com- modious lodging, ſtore of victuals, and ſuch other re- ſpects, not to be eſteemed of, but worthy great reprehen- ſion. Therefore it is requiſite he practiſe himſelfe firſt of all to be a perfect priuate Souldier, before he be drawne to the deſire of bearing office, which were to ſet the cart before the horſes, and worke by contraries : for firſt wee muſt learne to obey, and then it is lawfull to gouerne. But it is no new thing, nor to be maruelled at, that ſome men are accuſtomed to obtaine charges by vnlawfull and indirect meanes, I will not ſay, that they vſe them accor- dingly. Therefore to merite a charge, it is alwaies farre more excellent and more conuenient to winne them by deſert, then to enter thereinto by intruſion : for thoſe that doe not begge them doe feele in themſelues their proper ſufficiencie : where contrariewiſe they are a heauie bur- then to thoſe that know them not, although with great inſtance they haue procured and ſought for them. Which

E   **want**

want and vnwarie dealing in this our age, peraduenture proceedes of the small neede the world seemes to haue of good Souldiers at this day, and of the little experience moft men in our time haue of the Art of warre or at leaftwife our Superiours are blinded with the fweete baites of couetoufneffe, cheife caufe of fuch elections. Yet this notwithftanding we ought to retaine with all reuerence, the honour and credite due to an expert and good Souldier, who with diligence being fought for and felected, as neere as is poffible, ought to haue the moft chofen charges, and expeditions giuen to their gouernment. To the end thofe affaires may fall out happily, to the honour of their Nation and profit of their Prince. Whilft he doth follow the warres, or is in Campe: let him carrie as little baggage with him as is poffible, that he may be the more nimble and light of body, fpeedy in his iourney or marching, and the more apt for all enterprifes.

During the warres (or elfe not) he ought to weare in fome conuenient place of his garments, that is moft apparant to the view of the band, a token, red croffe, or fcarfe, whereby in skirmifhes and other attempts he is to be knowne of what part he is (the Emperials vfe a red fcarfe, Englifhmen *Saint Georges Croffe*, the French the *White-croffe*, &c.) or fuch a figne as the Generall of the field fhall make choife of, which he ought to do willingly, thereby to remoue fufpition out of the minde of his Captaine and Cheifteines, that they need not to ftand in doubt of him : and for diuers other worthy refpects, fince that by thefe and like manifeft meanes, the Souldier fhewes inward faith and loialty to the Officers and Captaines which gouerne. But if otherwife they carrie the

said

said token and marke loose at their necke, breast, armes, or any other place, it giues matter and occasion of doubt touching their fidelitie: specially being but newly entertained, since that being not made fast, they may easily cast away or hide the same in time of perill or doubtfull fight: Which suspition ought diligently to be remoued by him which carrieth an entire desire and full intent to deale truely and loially.

He ought likewise to beware, vnder paine of great punishment, for running from one campe to another, for what occasion soeuer shall vrge him to it, but is bound to serue that partie with which hee doth first place himselfe, euen vntill the end of the wars.

I haue seene it likewise not lawfull, that a Captaine should receiue into his seruice a Souldier that is departed from another Captaine of the same faction, and this was obserued, to the end that Souldiers should be kept obedient and stedfast vnder their Ensigne, where first they haue placed themselues. Prouided alwaies, that their Captaines intreat them honestly and well, which is to be decided by the Marshall of the field. Neuerthelesse, so often as a Souldier is forced of necessitie to leaue the warres, he ought not to depart out of his seruice, but by the speciall licence of his Captaine, accompanied with an autentike pasport of his good seruice, so shall he shun many confusions which are great occasions of scandals and infinite troubles, by meanes whereof he may freely make relation of the good seruice he hath done, and boldly shew himselfe before any mans face.

He ought to take speciall care, that he be not the beginner and occasion of any discords and mutinies, neither consent thereunto, what reason soeuer should lead

E 2   him

him therennto, since that such peruerse proceeding doth not agree with the worthy, noble, and famous Art of warre, which is a dangerous discredite to such malefactors, and for the most part without any recouery doth procure the generall ruine of many valiant Captaines and mighty armies. And therefore Ruffians and common Hackers that liue idle in the streetes at home, and follow the wars onely for spoile, are most vnfit to make Souldiers, for experience makes manifest, that they are the onely cause of mutinies, so that one such is able to corrupt and disorder a whole band. Wherefore a good Souldier ought rather to apply himselfe to suffer things impossible, then commit so great an error, for by the one great honour and praise shall redound vnto him, and by the other vile act, he shall gaine manifest blame and assured death : for such notable errors, without any remission, or any pitie (as in part I haue before touched, and hereafter in the marshall lawes shall set downe) are seuerely to be chastised.

When the Companie doth disband, and euery souldier is to go to his lodging or cabbin, it is very requisite hee stay vntill such time as he see the Ensigne lapt vp and lodged, to the intent, if he be of the gard about the same, that night he may attend to doe his dutie, otherwise hee may lawfully depart, and thereby shunne the shamefull name of a stubborne, licentious and disobedient person. He must learne to vnderstand the assured sound of the drumme, thereby to know alwaies whereunto he is appointed, and what thing is to be done and obeied, which of duty is accustomed to be done, since that with this instrument Souldiers are giuen to vnderstand, during the warres, what things be necessarie to be executed : One
thing

thing befides is moft neceffarie for a Souldier, which is, that he learne perfitly to fwimme, both for that waters cannot alwaies be paffed with wading, neither at all times boates and bridges can be conueied with the campe, by reafon of naughtie paffages, as alfo in diuers enterprifes a man is both more fafe and more bold, knowing what he can doe: whereof young *Shelley* made a moft famous proofe, who at the victualing of *Midleborow*, when their nauie was affaulted by the *Flufhingers*, hauing all his companie flaine, fwam a fhore with his armes, being the laft man left aliue a fhipbord: and as the *Spaniards* at the paffage of the arme of the fea, when they went to befiege *Siricke-fea*. Befides the notable attempt made at the great riuer of *Alba* in *Saxonie*, the yeere 1547. where the Imperialifts had fo famous a victorie.

Now therefore let no man perfwade himfelfe, that the feuerall and particular experience which belongs to a perfect good Souldier, can be perfectly and duely obtained by any other way, but by a continuall delight, exercife, and obferuation. For no man doth bring any worke to perfection, whereof he hath not the Art: euery Art doth fpring of experience and knowledge, and knowledge doth arife by meanes of ftudie and continuall practife. Military profeffion being then more perfect and aboue all other Arts, confequently it is neceffarie wee vfe in the fame greater ftudie, and more continuall exercife then is to be vfed in any other Art: for fo much as it is a moft auncient and prudent fentence: All arts doe confift in exercife: and therefore continually at idle times it is very fit and neceffarie for a fouldier, to practife and exercife himfelfe amongft his Companions in the campe, in running, leaping, throwing the barre, or fuch like, to make

E 3 him

him actiue, and to auoide ſuch idle paſtimes as Souldiers commonly now adaies vſe, contrarie to all good
order.

Beſides which, as I haue partly touched before, euery
priuate Souldier ought not onely to be well able to vſe
the weapon hee ſerueth withall, but alſo ſuddainely to
vnderſtand all commandements of his Gouernors, whether it be by voice or ſound of drumme or otherwiſe, and
to know how to maintaine himſelfe in order without
breaking aray, not onely marching, but alſo turning in a
troupe or retiring. For that Souldier which knoweth his
dutie how to behaue himſelfe in the campe, in watch,
ſcout &c. and likewiſe in marching, turning, retiring,
and fighting or skirmiſhing to obſerue the order pre-
ſcribed by his Captaiue, may be called a trained and old
Souldier: Whereof if he be ignorant, although he haue
beene twentie yeares in the warres, he is not to be eſteemed a Souldier. But in theſe exerciſes the Sergeants and
Officers are daily and duely to inſtruct generally and
priuately each ſouldier, which Officers ought of neceſſity to haue knowledge in reading, that both what is written before, and ſhall be written after in this booke, ſpecially touching the Marſhall lawes of the fielde, they may
euer read as a Lecture to their ſouldiers, being in *corps de
gard*, or at other fit and conuenient times. For theſe be
things ſo neceſſarie to be knowne and obſerued, that it
doth both import very much that each ſouldier ſhould
haue them by heart, and if it were poſſible, ſowed vpon
their garments to be a perpetuall glaſſe to looke into,
whereby they might guide all their actions, that thereby
they might ſee what they ought to ſhunne for feare of
puniſhment, and what to imbrace to increaſe credit.

To

To knit vp this our firft difcourfe, he that findes himfelfe fufficient and well inclined to exercife this moft excellent profeffion, ought with all modeft humilitie , and
good intention, frame himfelfe to a perfect obedience,
afwell to obferue order, a thing fo conuenient and neceffarie in this exercife , as alfo to execute that which fhall
be commanded him by his Captaine.

Before a Souldier binde himfelfe to ferue in a band, he
ought aduifedly to confider, and exprefly to perfwade
himfelfe, that vnder an expert, valorous, and worthy
Captaine, feldome or neuer our trauaile in well doing is
forgotten or loft : when as the contrarie doth chance vnder thofe that be vaine, vicious, and of fmall experience,
who through want of perfection and practife, doe not
know the merit of the valiant and valorous acts of a good
Souldier : fo that confequently they neglect all toile and
trauell done in any honourable enterprife. Therefore
it behoues a Souldier to make a good choife at the firft,
for after whatfoeuer he be, he muft ftill obey him : and
likewife alwaies haue refpect, and carrie a reuerence to
the iuftice of Marfhall law, and the Minifters of the fame,
though they be of bafe condition, fince both by the law
of Nature and Nations, they ought to be obeyed and obferued, and particularly knowne, and had in memory of
euery priuate fouldier : for thereby both horfemen and
footemen are kept in perfect order.

But aboue all things a fouldier ought not to forget his
dutie and deuotion towards the goodneffe of our Lord
God, and our facred Chriftian religion, by which the true
gift of vertue, valour and fortitude , and all good things
befide, we moft certainely receiue, and are affured to attaine whilft our determinations be lawfull and honeft.

And

And for that a ſouldier being ſubiect to a thouſand daily dangers, it behoues him continually to liue as he dare die, and oftentimes to reconcile himſelfe to God by confeſſion of his ſinnes, and receiue the benefit of the moſt bleſſed Sacrament.

I haue beene ſomewhat more copious in this firſt diſcourſe touching a ſouldier, then perchance I meane to be in any of the reſt, by reaſon this is the firſt ſteppe and degree a man ought to ſet his feete vpon, before he mount the throne of perfect gouernment in Marſhall affaires: for if a ſouldier can obtaine tried experience in this firſt point, he may with more eaſe aſcend the other, ſince this is onely the ground worke of all the reſt.

CHAP. II.

The Office which appertaines to a Corporall, Cape de Squadre, Diſnier, or chiefe of Chamber.

IT is not to be doubted, but that all notable errors depend onely of idleneſſe, and that all worthy and commendable acts ſpring of vigilant warineſſe. Therefore a Corporall, Cape de Squadre, Diſnier, or chiefe of Chamber, or how you liſt to terme them, ought to be no leſſe prudent and carefull ouer the gouernment of his people, then a father in ruling of his family : and as euery parent doth paſſe in age his children, euen ſo a Corporall ſhould be ſuch, that he may exceede any ſouldier, if not by experience and yeeres, at leaſtwiſe with diligence and ſharpneſſe of wit. Through which endeauour and exerciſe, ioyned with a feruent deſire and delight, to attaine to the

perfit

perfit tip of this honourable profeffion, he fhall euery
day become more capeable, and of greater experience:
wherefore I would as neere as is poffible, not onely haue
him exprefly acquainted with the aduertifements and
Martiall lawes following, but alfo indued with the beft
of thofe conditions which I haue fet out in my former
difcourfe of a priuate Souldier, fince that to mount vp
to this fecond degree, it is very neceffary and requifite,
that he haue made long abode in the practife and experience in the firft ft p of feruice appertaining to a priuate
Souldier. The Captaine muft felect and choofe toure of
the moft skilfull Souldiers, which be honeft, loyall, and
perfect religious Chriftians, out of euery Hu dreth in
his band: whereof two are to haue charge of the fhot,
the oth r two of the pikes, euery one guiding 24. a piece,
the which ought all of them to be lodged together, and
the Corporall himfelfe in the middeft of his charge, wher-
by when any fecret feruice is to be done, they may call
and affemble by the appointment of the Superiour officers, their whole fquadron, or what leffe number elfe,
without the found of any drumme.

Now then a Corporall with his fquadron of 25. or
more, according to the difcretion of the Captaine, lodging together with his company, muft prouide generally
for all their reafonable wants of wages, match, pouder,
and other munition, and muft inftruct them how to handle their weapons. He muft likewife remember perfectly how euery one is armed and furnifhed when he receiu-
eth them in charge, and to fee that no part thereof be
fpoiled but preferued neat and trimme: and aboue all
things to looke well to the behauiour of his companie,
not fuffering them to vfe vnlawfull and prohibited gam-
F   ing,

ing, neither to giue themselues to drinking and surfeting, but to spare of their pay to furnish themselues brauely and surely against the enemie, wherein he ought to vse his chiefe indeauour. And if it happen that any fault is committed, his part is not violently to punish the Souldier himselfe, as hereafter is touched : but to make it knowne to his Captaine, who must not neither, as some rashly do, reuenge himselfe, but communicate the same with the Marshall or his Prouost, who onely haue vnder the Generall authoritie to punish : and this due course of iustice shall be more terrible to the Souldier, and breed lesse euill-will in them to the Captaine and Officers : generally in these respects, the Corporall must touching the foresaid causes or such like, or if any Souldier be sicke, hurt, or absent, by way of imprisonment or death, immediately make report thereof, finding any thing worthy relation, and spare no man, but deliuer ouer the truth to the Sergeant, the Sergeant from him, or together with the Corporall to the Lieutenant, and he or they all iointly to the Captaine, who is to take order in the cause. Thus shall dignitie of Officers be maintained, and Officers and faults redressed, to the great example of the euill, and comfort of the good. But somewhat more amply to set downe the foresaid respects together with certaine other aduertisements. A Corporall must alwaies fore-see and examine, that the souldiers of his Squadron keepe their armes in order, cleane and intire : and the Hargabusiers stored with match, bullets and pouder, and such like necessaries : a thing worthy to be noted and obserued in this profession : the which makes shew that the same is of a good souldier not onely vsed in time of warre, but in all other times and places, being a knowne difference

betwixt

betwixt the legitimate, and leud Profeſſors of armes. He ought of neceſſity ſtill to inſtruct and exhort them , that they liue together friendly, without diſcord : that they be modeſt and ſparing in their victuals , profitable in their apparell, and that generally they doe ſhun ſwearing, and blaſpeming vpon greeuous puniſhment, by which act of blaſpheming and ſwearing by the holy name of the ſacred Trinitie, they commit greater villany and offence before God , then if before the world they did commit moſt wicked acts , or infinite errors. Likewiſe let him prohibite all vnlawfull games , for the performance whereof he ought to proceede with as great dexteritie and curteſie as he can, that alway in matters of importance, he may haue that due obedience which is required, and not through crueltie gaine the hate and euill-will of thoſe perſons, which in many other things beſide are to obey him : for to chaſtiſe them, lies neither in his power, neither in the arbitriment of other Officers , although they be of degrees higher then he , but doth iuſtly appertaine to the Office of the Maſter of the Campe, and Marſhall of the field. The which point is to be noted and obſerued, to the diſcredite of ſome Captaines , which at this day delight to imbrew their murthering hands in the bloud of ſouldiers, and men perchance of honeſt behauiour, being moued thereunto through ſome hatred, toy, or beaſtly paſſion.

Therefore he muſt alwaies be mindfull to obſerue this honourable rule of diuers good and diſcreet Officers, who ſometimes doe ouer-ſee and winke at light faults, and proceed with a certaine modeſtie and lenitie , although in matters of greater inſolencie, with ſeueritie.

Notwithſtanding theſe and ſuch like authorities , the

Corpo-

Corporall ought to be no leſſe obedient to euery leaſt point of the Marſhall lawes : and in ranke and aray, or in other places where thoſe of greater gouernment be, he muſt performe and obſerue the part and dutie of a priuate Souldier, and retaine like order and obedience : for where our betters be, the leſſe giue place.

But when alone with his ſquadron he is conducted to the place where he is to make watch and ward : then muſt he take vpon him his office, and make prouiſion of wood or coles, that he may alwaies haue fire burning in his corps of gard, aſwell in the day as in the night, and aſwell in the ſummer as in the winter : without which hee ought neuer to keepe watch, becauſe it is a moſt neceſſarie munition for the Hargabuſiers, to light their match withall, and for other needfull reſpects. Likewiſe hee muſt prouide for oyle, for candles for the night time, for lant-hornes and ſuch like at the Sergeant Maiors hands, or of ſome others, who haue charge to prouide for thoſe things, and are accuſtomed to diſtribute the ſame. If hee keepe his corps de gard in an open and plaine place or otherwiſe : he muſt conforme the company of his ſquadron, according to the order appointed by his betters: and with the moſt ſpeedy and artificiall manner that he can, muſt arme and fortifie with ditches, trenches, and ſentinels, the place where he muſt make his abode with this his ſmall band and troupe of ſouldiers, the better to reſiſt the enemies furie, or any ſurpriſe he might aſſault him withall, conſidering that ſometimes, yea and that very often, being ſet vpon, the Sentinels and corps de gard be repulſed and haue their throates cut, to the great diſturbance and vniuerſall domage of the whole Campe. He muſt ordaine his watch in ſuch a place, that in the ſame at
all

all times he may remaine warie and vigilant, placing himfelfe in the moft high and eminent feate of all the corps de gard, to the intent that hee may know and difcerne in due time euery particular accident that fhall happen or fucceede : and thereof immediately aduertife his Captaine of all, that he may prouide remedy with fpeed, according as the cafe requires warily and fecretly, euen at the clofing of the night, vntill the bright fpring of the *Diana,* and faire day-light : he muft ordaine and place Sentinels, and often fearch and vifite them, with the aide of two of the Captaines Gentlemen of his company, called of the *Italians Lanže Spezzate,* or might be tearmed more aptly, extraordinarie Lieutenants, that he may alwaies remaine vigilant and affured, to the intent he be not affailed vnprouided, to his great domage, and before he can giue warning of the enemie to the campe, which doth reft and lie in fafetie in that quarter where he is, vnder his charge, care, and diligence. In fuch cafes he ought therefore to imploy the beft men he hath, that hee neuer reft deceiued in a matter of fo great importance, fince that of thofe which be but meane Souldiers, or as I may well tearme them, negligent perfons, nothing elfe is to be looked for at their hands, but error, loffe, and danger.

Moreouer he muft at the leaft caufe the third part of his fquadron to remaine and ftand continually armed at all points, both night and day, confifting of greater or leffe quantity of people, according as the fufpition doth argue the neede of them to be fmall or great : the Hargabufiers hauing their flaskes and furniture tied to their girdles, and their peeces ready charged, that vpon a fuddaine they may contend by skirmifh, according to need-

F 3 full

full occaſion, and readily reſiſt the enemie without ſlacking or any remiſſion of time, vntill all the ſquadron be put in order.

He muſt be very circumſpect, that the reſt of the ſouldiers weapons, and principally his owne, be laid vp and placed in ſuch order, one kinde being diuided from another, that in one inſtant they may be ſpeedily and readily armed: the which he muſt daily put in practiſe, and inure them withall, by fained alarmes, by ſpeciall commandement and of ſet purpoſe, which be moſt neceſſarie to be practiſed before hand for diuers honourable and important reſpects, worthy to be had in good conſideration.

Therefore let him haue and carie a continuall care, that their armes neuer remaine in any confuſed order, the which if he ſhould ſuffer, he ſhould find no doubt to be a great want: but the ſame may be preuented, and made eaſie, by accommodating the Hargabuſiers in rancke one by one, vpon a boord or banke: the Pikes and Corſlets, in order reared and hanged vpon ſome wall or other apt place in the corps de gard, and vpon each particular weapon and peece, euery ſouldier ſhould haue a proper and ſpeciall marke before hand made whereby to know the ſame. He ought daily to inſtruct his ſquadron euery one apart, how to handle the weapon wherewith they ſerue: the Hargabuſier to charge and diſcharge nimbly, the Pikeman to toſſe his pike with great dexteritie.

Sentinels ought with great reaſon to be placed about the corps of gard, to the intent the ſame may be defended and kept with more ſafety and ſecuritie. Hee himſelfe at the cloſing of the night, muſt place the firſt Sentinell, and ſo conſequently the reſt, inſtructing them orderly what manner they haue to obſerue, and how they

ought

ought to gouerne themfelues in fuch accidents as might
infue : who are to remaine in Sentinell in winter and cold
weather, but one houre, or two at the moft : but in fom-
mer, two or three houres before they be changed : for
which refpect,that euery one may be taxed with æquity,
let him firft make a iuft diuifion of his number, according
to the number of the houres in the night , and following
that proportion, let him fee the fame performed, without fauouring or omitting any , the which hee may the
more certainely performe, if the names of his Souldiers
be written in a roll, and when the houre glaffe hath runne
their time (which is neceffarie for him to haue in his
corps de gard) then to pricke their names, and place new
in their roomes, fo fhall each Souldier be partaker of the
trauaile, and reft maruelloufly well fatisfied. But for that
in wars, canuifados, furprifes , fallies, fuch like cafualties
and aduertifements be infinite, I will leaue the reft to his
owne vigilant difcretion, and fuppofe it needleffe to aduertife him of euery particular point ; more then that I
haue and will touch in this my firft booke of *Militarie directions*, as cafes moft proper for priuate Souldiers. I
therefore at this prefent thinke it fufficient for a Corporall to know, that it is neceffarie he fhould fo difpofe the
matter through his prouident prouifion , that all his people may be reduced into order, and already haue taken
their weapons in their hands , before the enemie giue
charge vpon them. And therefore in time and place of
fufpition and danger, he muft place loft Sentinels without the watch-word, a good diftance off, from the corps
de gard, in places moft fufpect. But in other places not
needfull fo much to be fufpected,and that be neerer him,
he ought to fet Sentinels with the watch-word , fo farre
one

one from an other, as it ſhall ſeeme vnto him reaſonable or requiſite, and that they may inuiron the ground one within the ſight of an other, or ſo that the enemy cannot enter, or any eſpion iſſue without their knowledge. If great occaſion ſo demaund, let him place together one Hargabuſier, and one armed Pike, to the intent that the one may keepe the enemie farre off, and in a certaine ſort ſuſtaine his fury at the point of his pike, whilſt the Hargabuſier with the diſcharge of his peece, giues Arme to the corps de gard and campe, which exploit may be the better performed, if a corporall-ſhippe of Pikemen bee ioyned together with an other of ſhot. Sometimes without making any noyſe or rumour, Arme is giuen to the campe, for one of the two Sentinels may retire, and make relation to the Corporall what hath appeared, been ſince, heard or happened, whereby he may ſpeedily with great ſilence giue Arme to the gard, without leauing the place of the Sentinell diſarmed, which they ought neuer to a-bandon, but at ſuch times as the enemie is maniteſtly diſcouered, the occaſion of the alarme being certaine, at which time being retired, they muſt vnite themſelues to-gether with the ſouldiers of the gard, that they may all wholy in one company execute that which ſhall fall out beſt for their purpoſe, which is, to retire fighting or skir-miſhing to the campe, according to ordinarie cuſtome, notwithſtanding by the order and appointment of thoſe which haue authority to commaund them, as their Cap-taine, Sergeant maior, &c. but neuer otherwiſe.

He ought moreouer to be circumſpect, that in the bo-dy of the watch a ſolemne ſecret ſilence be kept, without ſinging, brawling, or any rumour or noiſe, and ſpecially in the night, both in reſpect of the enemie, to heare when

the

the alarme is giuen, and to the intent that thofe which reft and fleepe, and are not yet in *Sentinell*, may be the more apt to refift and apply themfelues to thefe actions and exercifes, which are required of them with vigilant watchfulneffe, fince a man cannot without great difficultie remaine without fleepe or reft, any much longer time then our nature is accuftomed by ordinarie courfe to beare, and therefore at the entrance of the corps de gard, he ought likewife to keepe a proper Sentinell appertaining to the gard, that neither friend nor enemie comming out of the campe or elfewhere, fhall be able to enter without yeelding the watch-word : and in this fort muft the Corporall proceed, euen vntill the diana bee founded through all the Campe. For other refpects, I finally referre him to my following difcourfe , which together with that written before , it is requifite he haue in perfit memorie as well as the priuate fouldier.

Chap. III.
Six fpeciall Points appertaining to Souldiers of all forts.

IT is written in the hiftory of *Pietro Bizari*, touching the incredible and maruellous obedience of the Turkifh fouldiers, that a certaine Gentleman at his returne from *Conftantinople* did declare vnto the Earle of *Salma*, that he had feene foure miracles in the Turkifh dominions : Which was, firft an infinite armie almoft without number, confifting of more then foure hundred thoufand men. Secondly, that amongft fo many men, he faw

G not

not one woman. Thirdly, that there was no mention made of wine. And laſt, at night when they had cried with a hie-voice *Alla*, which is *God* : there continued ſo great a ſilence through the whole campe, that euen in the pauilions they did not ſpeake but with a low ſoft voice, a thing werthy to be admired,to the great ſhame of Chriſtians : therefore if the Infidels obſerue ſuch ſtrict diſcipline, why ſhould not weę that be Chriſtians indeauour our ſelues to ſurpaſſe them therein ? recommending our ſelues and affaires to God, with reuerence and ſilence, which I would wiſh to be continued vntill the diana, when together with the ſound of the drummes, the ſame might be with a cheerefull crie renued. But together with ſilence to ſet downe certaine other vertues, take them here as I finde them written.

Silence.

In all places of ſeruice ſuch ſilence muſt be vſed, that ſouldiers may heare friends, and not be heard of enemies, as well in watch, ward, ambuſh, canuiſado, or any other exploit : in which point conſiſteth oftentimes the ſafety or perdition of the whole campe.

Obedience.

Such obedience muſt be vſed, that none regard the perſons but the office to them appointed, diligently obſeruing the ſame : any offending to the contrary, running into the danger of the law, for longer then obedience is vſed and maintained, there is no hope of good ſucceſſe.

SECRET-

SECRETNESSE.

Souldiers muſt be ſecret, and haue regard that they diſcloſe nothing, though ſometimes they vnderſtand the pretence of the higher powers. The Diſcloſers of ſuch, merite moſt cruell puniſhment.

SOBRIETY.

In Sobriety conſiſteth great praiſe to the ſouldiers, who vſing the ſame are euer in ſtate of preferment, ſuch regard their duties, and reproue the raſh Buſi-bodies, Drunkards, &c. are euer in danger of puniſhment.

HARDINESSE.

The Captaines and ſouldiers that be hardy of courage, be much auaileable in ſeruice, ſpecially ſuch as will ponder what may be the end of their enterpriſe. Some in times paſt haue hardly giuen the onſet, and after repented the ſame: but the praiſe of the aduiſed cannot bee expreſſed.

TRVTH and LOYALTY.

The vertue of Loyaltie and Truth is farre exceeding my capacitie to write, the Practiſers of the contrary are not worthy of life, but to be ſoone adiudged. Subtile enemies approue to corrupt ſouldiers with gifts, and the Deuill to entrap them with the ſweete intiſing baites of leud libertie. But ſince the reward of truth is euerlaſting

G 2   life,

life, and the vntrue and diffembler loofeth the fame in continuall darkneffe, I truft none of our Countrey-men will learne the one for the other, will be falfe to his Soueraigne, or flee from the affured piller of the true faith : from which God keepe all good fouldiers.

Chap. IV.

How a Souldier may maintaine obedience, and keepe himfelfe in the fauour and good grace of his Captaine.

A Good Souldier ought to haue confideration, that fince due orders and lawes are the affured foundation and ftay of euery ftate : and contrariwife, difcord and difobedience the ruine of all Realmes : fo that aboue all things a well gouerned Generall, and a carefull Captaine, ought prudently to fore-fee that their Campe and Souldiers be paid and punifhed with equall execution of iuftice, not refpecting perfon : yeelding to the Offenders punifhment, and reward to the vertuous : depreffing vice, and exalting vertue : vfing commendation to the good, and correction to the euill, ioyned with admonifhments of magnanimitie, the which if they preuaile not, to chaftife them : and as the good hufband doth plucke the weedes out of the good corne, to the intent that they by their wicked and pernicious example, do not infect the reft, and confequently doth prouide that no fault paffe vnpunifhed, nor no valorous act vnrewarded : by which meanes he becomes feared, fauoured, obeyed, and beloued of all the armie : euen fo on the other fide, the good natured fouldier muft euer haue refpect to keepe the
bondes

bondes of modefty towards his Superiour, and yeelde many thankes to God, that he hath giuen him fo iuft and vertuous a Captaine and Generall , towards whom hee muft alwaies yeeld like obedience, that the fonne doth to the father, being bound fo to doe by the diuine law,without fhewing himfelfe oppofite to the order of generall iuftice, nor vngratefull for his receiued benefits, but continually by his good guiding in the one and the other, giue his Captaine iuft caufe to loue and like well of him.

Souldiers be euer bound to obey the iuftice and commandements of their Superiours : and the Superiour likewife to embrace the obedience of his Souldiers, whilft he doth fee himfelfe honoured and obeyed of them, either in deedes or words,in earneft or diffembling.

Although the Generall or Captaine were a right *Sardanapalus*, fo that his lawes be obeyed all things fall out well : wherefore a Souldier ought with all his indeauour to be obedient to the law, with his whole heart loue his Captaine, and feare him with all his force.

Cyrus being cruell, couetous, miferable,and an Exacter of taxes, through iuftice was beloued and obeyd.

Cambyfes, Marcus Cato, and *Marcus Antonius* , the two firft being feuere and cruell, yet amongft the Souldiers were maruelloufly fauoured : and the third, although hee was drowned in the deepe and gaping gulfe of Lechery, Gluttony, and riotous gaming, yet was he fo beloued of his armie, that his Souldiers would haue fuffered themfelues to be crucified, to haue done any thing gratefull vnto him, and that cheifly through his iuftice : and therefore it behoues a Souldier to keepe inuiolate the Martiall lawes of the field. But to touch the cheifeft meanes whereby a Souldier may be drawne to obey, to feare, and loue the Captaine, and altogether gaine his good liking and fauour, carie in minde what infueth.

Firſt, a Souldier muſt preſume and perſwade himſelfe, that whatſoeuer he doth in ſecret, that it ſhall come to the knowledge of the Captaine, whether it be good or euill: which feare if he be wiſe, will reſtraine him from doing any thing pernicious, or againſt the Marſhall law, or the miſliking of the Captaine, and ſo ought to reſt in continuall doubt, leſt his euill deedes come to light, and to the eares of the ſuperiour Officers, that with the ſword of iuſtice, the rod of reuenge, and the ſcepter of rule, may and will chaſtice him. If he remember this, no doubt he will liue modeſtly, in obſeruing thoſe lawes which are commanded by the Captaine and Generall: for it behoues a ſouldier ſtill to liue in ſuſpect, that ſpials and intelligencers be euer preſent at his elbow, which no doubt will accuſe him for his euill behauiour: of which ſort a Captaine and Generall haue great ſtore to keepe the Campe and Souldiers in continuall ſuſpicion and feare.

A Souldier muſt euer ſhew himſelfe gratefull to his Captaine in words and deeds, by remaining patient in his actions, and not to vſe complaints in his ſpeeches ſuffering with quiet contentation the penurie of victuals, if the Campe ſhould want, either through fault of the Generall, bareneſſe of the Countrey, or otherwiſe by his negligence, or through the malignitie of fortune, that neither by water nor land corne and victuals can be brought to them in ſafetie: wherefore we muſt weare out this want patiently, and not with a melancholike countenance, make appearance of a wrathfull and furious perſon, by charging of the Chiefetaine openly with thoſe

wants:

wants: for which proceeding, let him affure himfelfe that
he fhall be efteemed of euery man an infolent, feditious,
and impatient fouldier. Murmure not againft thy Captaine with thy tongue, but rather lament in thy heart thy
euill fortune, refting content with that portion of victuals
his Sergeant fhall giue thee for that day. Seeme ioyfull
whilft thy Captaine is merry, and forrowfull when he is
grieued, yeelding comfort and confolation, together
with faithfull counfell, as the caufe requireth.

Shew not thy felfe full of wrath and malcontent, for
want of thy wonted pay, although thou manifeftly perceiue the fame to proceed of the couetoufneffe of thy
Captaine: but diffemble and fhew him fo gratefull a
countenance, that he thereby may be moued to pay the
band, if not all, at the leaft part. If thefe delayes proceed
not by his fault, and that therefore hee laments thy lingring want: make free offer vnto him to fuffer all lacke
and difcommoditie to pleafure him withall: whereby he
fhall be maruelloufly moued, and much more bound to
loue a curteous fouldier.

Doe not moleft him with demaunding more fuccour
and preft-money, then thou haft need of, yea and that
when needy force conftraines.

Report not any thing but that which is profitable and
beneficiall for the publike State: for otherwife thou fhalt
be accounted a malicious Detractour, infolent, and in-
fupportable, making rehearfall of euery little trifle, wher-
by hatred is gained in exchange of gaining fauour. Faile
neuer in the diligent execution of thy duty, and make
fhew of thy forwardneffe, euen purpofely with the firft,
euen in thofe things that appertaine not to thy charge.

Difobey not the Captaines or Generals precepts, nor
withftand

withstand the martiall lawes : neither affirme that any thing is euill wrought which is done, for it appertaines not to a souldier to reprehend : but to a Councellor to admonish. Do not importune thy Captaine to reward thy trauell and seruice, but attend his liberalitie : for if thou become importunate, he will likewise become *Marcus Crassus*, who at the first vsing great liberality, being continually and ouermuch craued, became at the last extreame couetous.

Present him neuer with any thing, specially with any thing of value : for thy captaine which hath no neede of that which is thine, and perceiuing thee to present him that which is not correspondent to the merite of his worthinesse will esteeme the same to be done in manner of merchandise, as proceeding of craft : but if thy Captaine demaund any thing vnder shew of praising and commending the same, or the beautie thereof, it is then requisite that the same be liberally bestowed vpon him, it being a curteous demaund, which hee commonly will magnificently recompence, as did *Artaxerxes*.

Accept neuer any thing of thy enemy souldier, neither receiue any letter, yea if it should be from thy father, without licence of thy Captaine Generall, as a thing which only appertaines to Councellors and Chieftaines : for thy Captaine would become iealous ouer thy fidelitie, suspecting that thou wert corrupted. There is another note, specially to aduertise all souldiers of, that they doe not rashly, neither of purpose disdaine to be gouerned and commaunded of a Captaine, which is perchaunce of no auncient house, as an infinite number of fond and presumptuous fellowes doe now adaies : who being rude and rusticall Clownes, disdaine to be guided by Captaines,

taines, whofe valour and vertue, and not whofe auncient
ftocke, hath giuen them that degree, being afcended to
fo high honour by the fteps of vertue : for I haue feene
fome that but lately haue left their nedles, their hammers,
and their fpades, hauing fcarce feene a fmall skirmifh, but
that they prefume themfelues to be expert Souldiers, and
will fay, what is my Captaines valour more then mine?
Is not he of bafe degree as well as I? not confidering that
we be all fprung out of one ftocke, but that our valour
and vertue hath made vs noble, as hath beene verified in
diuers Princes, Kings and Emperours, as *Caius Marius,*
Lucius Quintus Cincinatus, Attilius Collatinus, Valentinia-
nus, Maximinianus, Francifco Carmognuolo, Iulian Romero,
and *Mondragon,* befides diuers others moe, which at this
day doe liue, being exalted by the degrees and way of
vertue, to the tippe of fuch praife as is moft conuenient
to worthy Captaines : and therefore no fouldier ought to
difdaine to be gouerned by fuch, whofe vertue hath made
noble their mindes.

And moreouer, if any fuch a one that is become Captaine, either by meanes of fauour or vertue, bee blotted
with fome vice or defect, yet wee ought not to difobey
him : for *Cæfar* was ambitious, great *Alexander* a Drun-
kard ; *Hanniball* vnfaithfull, cruell, and without religion;
Fabius Maximus by lingring efteemed a Coward ; *Marcel-*
lus rafh and vnaduifed : And therefore although thy Captaine be accounted moft vicious yet if he know how to
gouerne and guide his charge, a fouldier muft obey him,
and neither calumnioufly reprehend him, nor corruptly
imitate and obferue his vices, but duely and directly fulfill his precepts : fo that no fouldier or Gentleman, of
what Great-houfe foeuer, ought to difdaine to be com-
H manded

manded of ſuch as haue riſen by vertue, to the height of
honour, neither any man, how great of linage ſoeuer he
be, to diſdaine to accept leſſe degrees then a Captaine.
For thoſe be the ſteps by the which he muſt aſcend vnto
higher dignitie, as many auncient and noble perſonages
haue done, who from inferiour degrees by little and little
haue come to ſuperiour, whereof the great Emperour
Caius Iulius Cæſar may be example: who being borne of
a noble houſe amongſt the *Romanes*, was firſt choſen
Pretor in *Spaine* (a baſe office in reſpeſt of his worthy
parentage) as being reputed vnworthy of any greater
office.

CHAP. V.

Martiall and Militarie lawes, whereunto Souldiers of all de-
grees muſt be ſworne, to keepe and maintaine inuiolated at
all times and in all places, whether they ſerue Emperour,
King or Prince.

1 FIrſt, he that contrary to the word of God (whom in
all our aſtions we muſt firſt haue reſpeſt vnto) doth
maintaine, perſwade, and fauour any infidelitie, hereſie,
ſchiſme, ſtrange or new religion whatſoeuer, and doth
not cleaue to the true Chriſtian faith, ſhall incurre the
law appertaining.

2 *Item* that thoſe which without the feare of G O D
deſpiſe and deride his holy word, be puniſhed accordingly.

3 *Item* that no man ſpeake againſt the Chriſtian catholike faith, neither write againſt the ſame.

4 *Item*

4 *Item* that no fouldier of whatfoeuer degree or office he be doe breake, fpoile, abufe or prophane any Church.

5 *Item*, that no fouldier omit or abfent himfelfe from diuine feruice, if his Princes vrgent affaires will admit him to be prefent.

6 *Item*, that all fouldiers obferue and keepe the precepts of the Church.

7 *Item*, that contrariwife, no man be fo hardy to outrage any Church-man, either in word, deed, or any other finifter meanes, but in liew thereof, carrie a reuerent refpect to all and euery of them.

8 *Item*, that in like fort no man go about to defloure, commit adultery or fornication, with virgins, wiues, or widowes, neither by force, neither by other accident (vnleffe the party were confenting, and the matter fecret, which neuertheleffe is not lawfull before the face of God) vpon paine of death without mercy.

9 *Item*, that no man fhall deftroy, ruinate, endomage, or fet onfire any facred place, without licence of the Captaine or Generall.

10 *Item*, together with thefe forefaid cafes, whofoeuer fhall blafpheme, reuile or horribly fweare by the Almighty name of God, by his diuine Word and Sacraments, let fuch a peruerfe, impious and blafpheming perfon be punifhed openly, and to the terrour of the reft let it be executed: for no doubt the plague of the higheft will not depart from the tents of blafphemers and defpifers of religion: for how fhould wee vfe iuftice indifferently vnto men, when we are content with filence to fuffer fuch iniurie to be committed againft God? Therefore firft the offences done againft God muft be ftraightly pu-

H 2   nifhed

niſhed, and he then will giue thee wiſedome to decide the reſt, and triumphant victorie ouer thine enemies.

11 *Item*, all ſouldiers in generall, hauing taken their oath to ſerue God and aduance his word, they ſhall then next be ſworne to be true, iuſt, and dutifull to their Lord and Soueraigne, and his graund Generall, or chiefe Captaine of the field, to be tractable and obedient vnto euery Officer placed and appointed to rule ouer him, and to be ready both day and night to ſerue, whether it be by land or by water, as occaſion of ſeruice ſhall fall out and require: and whoſoeuer doth repine or ſheweth diſobedience herein, of what degree or condition ſoeuer he be, he muſt be duly puniſhed by the iudgement of the Superiours, appointed for that purpoſe.

12 *Item*, that whenſoeuer any Chieftaine or Captaine of any band, ſhall vpon vrgent cauſes appoint in his abſence any other whom he ſhall thinke good, to ſupply and execute his roome of Captainſhip; euery man ought to follow and obey the ſaid Deputie with no leſſe care and diligence, then they would the Captaine himſelfe vpon paine of ſuch puniſhment as the Generall or his aſſignes ſhall appoint.

13 *Item*, that all Souldiers muſt content themſelues with their places appointed, being ioyned together in bands, or ſeuerall without reſiſtance, whether it bee in marching, watching, incamping, or beſieging, being alſo commanded thereunto by the Captaine or other Officers, vpon ſuch paine as ſhall be thought good by the Captaine.

14 *Item*, that euery Souldier ſhall for his honour ſake, gladly fauour, and mercifully forbeare vnto the vttermoſt of his power all women lying in childbed, or being with child,

childe, or lately deliuered from childe, to defend and succour them from the rage of the cruell and rude souldiers, or others which follow the campe for spoile. Also it behoueth, as I said before, that all souldiers defend all Priests of godly calling, and all spirituall persons : but now adaies they be the first to whom abuse is offered, of what opinion or religion soeuer they be : but God no doubt will iustly plague all such before they be aware, and when they least suspect it.

15 *Item*, that euery souldier shall serue, and is by the law of armes bound by long custome to serue 30. daies for euery month, and after that rate he shall receiue his monthes wages.

16 *Item*, if that any souldier haue receiued his monthes wages aforehand , or any part thereof, and departeth without leaue or pasport from his CAP-TAINE , and hath not serued for it , he or they apprehended, shall for the said offence be aiudged to die.

17 *Item*, if there be any Souldier or Souldiers that in marching, breake his or their aray without iust occasion enforcing them, then the Prouost Marshall, Lieutenant of the band, or Sergeant, shall compell him or them with violence to keepe his or their ranckes in order : and if so be that he or they so disordered , doe chance in this case to be slaine, there shall no man bee blamed by his or their deaths, by the law of the field, for by such disordered people the whole armie may be in danger of ruinating by the enemie.

18 *Item*, if that by the appointment of the cheife RVLERS of the ARMIE , there bee a battaile fought , and that by the MIGHTY POWER OF GOD, the victorie be obtained on your side, the law

H 3 of

of armes is fuch, that if any fouldier hath receiued his monthes wages aforehand, he fhall be difcharged of the fame, neither fhall he ferue any longer for the faid wages, after the day of victory, neither fhall owe any thing for it, but he fhall be fet free from the months feruice.

19 *Item*, if it chance that in time of skirmifh, or in any other conflict with the enemie, fome one doe aduenture to flie and runne away from his Fellowes, if in the flying his Captaine or any other fouldier by fhooting at him, or by ftriking at him doe chance to kill him, they fhall incurre no danger for fo doing : and if fuch a flier chance to efcape at that time, and afterwards be taken, let him according to the law of armes fuffer death for the fame : for one fuch a Recreant may be the ouerthrow of a great multitude.

20 *Item*, it ftandeth with the law of armes, that each common fouldier fhall be fworne, that they will not haue amongft themfelues any priuate counfels, affemblies or conuenticles, vpon paine of the loffe of their liues.

21 *Item*, there fhall no fouldier, neither in time of marching, nor during the time of their incamping, hold or keepe any whifpering or talke, or fecretly conuey any letters vnto their aduerfaries, without licence from the chiefe Captaine, vpon paine of the loffe of his life.

22 *Item*, if there be any one, or more number, that fhall go about any treafon, or any other confpiracie to be committed againft the campe or garrifon, fuch a Traitor or confpirator fhall be accufed vnto the Knight Marfhall, and he that bewraieth and accufeth fuch an Offendor, fhall haue for his reward a monthes wages or more, as the fact is hainous : fo the reward is to bee increafed

vnto

vnto the partie that reuileth the fame, and the Offendor
to receiue the reward of a falfe Traitor.

23 *Item*, that no fouldier fhall be fuffered to bee of a
Ruffian-like behauiour, either to prouoke or to giue any
blow or thruft, or otherwife wilfully ftrike with his dagger, to iniury any his fellow-fouldiers with any weapon,
whereby mutinies many times enfue, vpon paine of the
loffe of his life.

24 *Item*, if any one beareth hatred or malice, or any
euill will for any occafion done vnto him, and fo ftriketh
him, he loofeth his hand, if otherwife he feeketh reuenge,
then by the law he loofeth his life.

25 *Item*, if any Souldier bee warned to watch and
ward, and he doe not come, he fhall be punifhed at the
difcretion of the Capraine : but if any fouldier be fum-
moned to watch, and he appeare, and after the watch-
word giuen, and the watch fet, he departeth and leaueth
the watch, fuch a one fhall without mercy be punifhed
with the loffe of his life : neither fhall any man fet an o-
ther to watch in his place without the leaue of the Captaine, vpon paine of his life.

26 *Item*, that no fouldier or fouldiers draw his or
their fwords, or vfe any other kinde of weapon, with
violence to doe hurt with, in or without the campe, during the time of the warres, vpon paine of death. It hath
lately beene vfed with more fauour of life, as fuch an
Offendor to loofe his hand : but it is the difcretion of
the Lord chiefe Generall, in whofe hands lieth both the
life and death of the Offendors after their arraignment
and iuft condemnation.

27 *Item*, the like law is againft the Officer and Officers of any band in the campe, if he ftrike any Souldier
without

without ſuch occaſion, as is permitted him in the articles to doe, otherwiſe he may defend himſelfe.

28 *Item*, that no perſon or perſons preſume to be
muſtered, or to take wages before hee be ſworne to bee
faithfull, and truely to ſerue his Prince in thoſe warres
preſent, vpon paine of death.

29 *Item*, that the Harold at armes ſhall proclaime
and publiſh all that the Generall ſhall giue him in charge,
in the place and places where he is commanded, and not
to adde or diminiſh any part or parcell thereof vpon
paine of death.

30 *Item*, there ſhall no Souldiers or other men, procure or ſtirre-vp any quarrell with any ſtranger, that is of
any other nation and ſuch as ſerue vnder one head and
Lord with them, neither in their gaming or otherwiſe,
vpon paine of the loſſe of his life.

31 *Item*, there ſhall no ſouldier or other perſon, being
in campe or march, take away any thing from any man
being their friend, by violence or deceipt, as their victuals
or other neceſſaries, vpon paine of the loſſe of his life.

32 *Item*, when there are any victuals carried or
brought vnto the campe, no man ſhall runne out to take
any part of them before they be brought to the appointed place for the purpoſe: no though they offer for them
more then they be worth, vpon paine of the loſſe of
his life.

33 *Item*, if that the Prouoſt Martiall haue at any time
taken an Offendor, and according to his office, he carieth
him to be puniſhed: and if that one or more Souldiers
ſeeke to reſcue the ſaid malefactor, and in this ſtirre the
Offendor eſcape, he or they that are the occaſion of this
eſcape, ſhall be puniſhed with the like puniſhment as
the

the Malefactor fhould haue beene, whether it be by life, or otherwife, according as the waight of the crime requireth.

34 *Item*, if there be any found, that hath entered his name vnder two Captaines, and hath taken wages, armour and weapons before-hand : fuch a perfon fhall be taken for a periured man, and by the law of armes, fhall for the fame lofe his life.

35 *Item*, if any man hath a place appointed him by the Harbinger or Officers for his tent or lodging, hee muft hold himfelfe content withall: neither fhall hee moleft any man lodging within his tent or cabbin, or other lodging at any time, for any occafion vpon paine of the chiefe captaines difpleafure, and fuch punifhment as he fhall thinke moft fit for the offence.

36 *Item*, that no man fhall found and make any alarme, except it be neede, or vpon commandment from the higher Officers, vpon paine of the loffe of his life.

37 *Item*, when of neceffitie the alarme is made, each man muft beftirre him to be ready for battaile, vpon paine of the loffe of his life.

38 *Item*, at the firft warning of the drumme or fecretly, all Souldiers muft be in a readineffe, and refort to the place appointed, which commonly is the market place (being firtt of all vnited with his Enfigne) and from thence in order of aray to the enemies, as they be commanded, vpon the paine of the loffe of his life.

39 *Item*, all fouldiers, being Horfemen or Footemen, muft diligently in order of aray by found of drum or trumpet, accompany the Enfigne to watch, ward, or releife of the fame, being there filently in a readineffe to withftand or difcouer the enemies : and as occafion fhall

I   ferue

serue to brute the alarme, with the vsuall word arme, arme, or bowes, bowes, if numbers or any bandes be in pay, vpon paine of losse of their liues.

40 *Item*, all souldiers must keepe their armour and weapons faire, cleane and seruiceable in a readinesse at euery sodaine, none intermedling but with his owne, euerie one to helpe other to arme, and diligently to resort to the place of seruice, at scrie, and larum vpon paine.

41 *Item*, all souldiers must honestly intreate, and truely pay Victuallers and Artificers, allowed for the releefe, being friends or enemies, and with curteous words encourage such to victuall, and releeue the companies or camp: vpon paine.

42 *Item*, all souldiers, in watch, ward, march, or otherwise, shall haue speciall regard, that if there be man or woman desirous to speake with the Superiours, or being thy enemies for feare doe forsake his owne power, and resort to thee : let such secretly be conueied to the Lord chiefe Generall, regarding that they view no secrets, least they be double spies vpon paine of the losse of their liues.

43 *Item*, Captaines and Officers, must oft frequent and resort vnto the Souldiers lodging to see in what state their armour and munitions be, and to giue great charge that their furniture be alwaies in a readinesse, the r corslets with all peices belonging to the same, and their caliuers to be made cleane and oiled, to haue match and pouder drie, bullets fit for their peeces, strings whipped for their bowes, their billes and halberds to be kept sharpe. And often to view euery particular vpon paine.

44 *Item*, he that shall depart out of the place where he shall be put, by his Head or any Officer whatsoeuer,

for

for a lost Sentinell, Spie, Watchman, Scout, or Warder, afwell by day as by night, as it often happeneth, to difco-uer fome dealings of the enemie, without attending and ftaying for him, that placed him there, to take him away, except he fhould remoue in haft to aduertife his head of the fucceffe of the enemies affaulting or doing any out-rage, fhall be punifhed with death.

45 *Item*, whofoeuer fhould rafhly offend or hurt, either in word or deeds, any man belonging to the Depu-ties or head Officers of iuftice or Captaine, there being in pay for Sergeants. And they being appointed to carrie no other weapon, with fteles or ftaues, but bills or hal-berds, they may be knowne for men of iuftice, and not for Souldiers.

46 *Item*. whofoeuer ftandeth within or without the campe or barres, to watch or fcout, and doth his dutie fo euill, that thorow his negligence, the enemie fetteth vpon the campe at vnawares, he fhall die.

47 *Item*, he that vnder colour of doing the dutie of a Scout or Spie, perceiuing the enemies haue affaulted the campe, and he with fuch faining lieth ftill, fhall die for it.

48 *Item*, he that fhall forfake the defence, in generall or particular, of the batterie, of the breach, of the paffage of a bridge, or other like to him committed, but lightly, not forced goeth away, fhall be for fo offending, pu-nifhed with death.

49 *Item*, whofoeuer entring into a Citie taken by force, followeth not his Enfigne whither foeuer it fhall go, vntill the Generall make Proclamation, that euery man fhall take booties: And if the Generall caufe no fuch Proclamation, to be made, and that fouldiers make

ſpoile, he ſhall incurre the paine of death, and if proclamation be made that they ſhall ceaſe from taking preies and booties, and after licence giuen, if they giue not ouer, they ſhall fall into the ſame puniſhment.

50 *Item*, whoſoeuer ſeeing the Enſigne, vnder the which he warreth in fraies or fight, by chance be falne in the handes of the enemies, if he be there preſent, and doe not his indeauour to recouer it, and when it is cowardly loſt, to puniſh the Souldiers which haue ſuffered it to be cowardly loſt, with death.

51 *Item*, he that ſhall flee from the battaile, being in the face and front of the enemies, or ſhall go ſlowly and ſlackly to ioyne, and afront with them, in caſe it be to fight a field battaile, or in any skirmiſh whatſoeuer, ſhall be puniſhed with death.

52 *Item*, he that ſhall faine himſelfe ſicke, to auoid the fighting of the enemie, or becauſe he would not go to any other enterpriſe to vſe his hands, but (I meane) therefor to rob, for to ſuch affaires they will bee ready enough, ſhall be cruelly puniſhed.

53 *Item*, whoſoeuer ſeeing his Generall, or his Captaine, or other Coronell, and Officer of the campe, in the hand of the enemies, and ſuccoureth him not with all his power, and may doe it, not reſpecting any danger, ſhall ſuffer death.

54 *Item*, he that ſhall rob or ſpoile the people of the Countrie, or Subiects, or Vaſſels of the Prince he ſerueth, ſhall die.

55 *Item*, he that by theft ſhould ſteale or rob the armour, weapons or horſes, or other thing from any other, ſeruing againſt the enemies, ſhall die.

56 *Item*, he that ſhould ranſome or taxe, or otherwiſe
miſ vſe

mif-vfe the people of the Countrie, except they fhould be enemies or rebels to the Prince, fhall bee greatly punifhed.

57 *Item*, he that fhall play at any game for his armor, weapons or horfes, which are written vpon the roll, or through his negligence fhall lofe them, or lend, giue a-way, or lay them to pawne, let him die.

58 *Item*, he that goeth further then two hundred fteppes or paces from his quarter, without licence of his Captaine, ipecially when the campe looketh or ftaieth to be affaulted by the enemies, except he fhould be fent for by his Heads, fhall be punifhed with death.

59 *Item*, he that fhall go longer then the houre ap-pointed in the night abroad, in the campe wandring, except he fhould be fent by his Superiours for a matter of weight, from head Captaine to head Captaine, by a counter-token, fhall be cruelly punifhed.

60 *Item*, he that fhall lodge ftrangers, whether he be of the campe or not, without licence of the Generall or of his Captaine, either in his lodging or vnder a tent, ex-cept he be of his chamber or fquadron, or by the Cap-taine appointed for feruice forth of the campe, fhall bee punifhed. But euery one ought to be in the night with their Camerads and chamber-fellowes, and not to be di-uided from their lodgings, that occafion feruing, they may be ready with their weapons in their hands: neither ought they to lodge watch, or fcoutes, or of the fearch: for that the Spies hauing no lodging, any excufe being found out, may the better be apprehended. Alfo if the Scout-watch be taken from their quarter, faining to be a fouldier of the campe when they are to fpie in the night: they for fo offending fhal be cruelly punifhed with death.

I 3

61 *Item*, whoſoeuer ſhall make any words, deedes, or queſtions in the ward, or in an ambuſh, or in other place, where reſpect and ſilence is needfull, ſhall be puniſhed.

62 *Item*, he that ſhould be reuenged of any iniurie receiued, either newly or before time done, by any indirect way: that is traiterouſly and not by way of reaſon, or by way of combate, body to body, by the licence of his Generall, ſhall ſuffer death.

63 *Item*, he that ſhould dare be ſo bold as to play with falſe cardes and dice, or ſhould vſe in play any priuie falſhood, theft or deceit in any wiſe, ſhall be puniſhed.

64 *Item*, he that of preſumption ſhould paſſe out of his place into another, either before the battell or in marching, ſhould out of order make haſt to go before, to be the firſt that ſhould come to the lodging of the campe, or in marching ſhould go out of his ranke from one battaile to another, or hee that doth not obſerue the order of marching, ſhall die.

65 *Item*, he that ſhall taske or ranſome vpon his Hoſt or Lodger, or vpon any other that is not his lawfull Priſoner by good order of warre, and that he is lawfully taken, the ranſome excell not the articles of agreement, that there bee a iuſt ranſome ſet, vpon paine of puniſhment.

66 *Item*, he that ſhall enter in, or go forth by any other gate, ſtreet or way, then that which ſhall bee accuſtomed, into the Citie, pales, or liſt, or fort, where the campe is lodged, that is going ouer the walles, or vnder ſome breach, and not by the ordinary gate, let him fall into the paine of death.

67 *Item*, whoſoeuer doth not immediately retire,

when

when he shall heare the trumpet or drumme, sound the retreat, either of a set battaile, or of a skirmish or battery, or of any other fight, or should go in or come forth of the City, when the assault is giuen to the walles thereof, shall die.

68 *Item,* he that speaketh, or calleth, or crieth aloud, amongst the ordinance, or in battaile, or in any place where silence needeth, except he were a Head, or other Officer, or Sergeant, commaunding some new order, shall die.

69 *Item,* he that shall commit any thing whatsoeuer it be, whereby it may be coniectured, that it is against the Prince, and domageable to the Generall and the campe, shall die.

70 *Item,* Drummes and Fifes must oft sound and exercise their instruments, warning as the mouth of man, to all points of seruice : so must souldiers diligently learne and obserue the meaning of the same, that none plead ignorance, neglecting their duties to seruice appertaining. Also sometimes they shall receiue from the higher Officers or Captaines, secret commaundements by word of mouth, the which must with all diligence be obserued, and truely executed vpon the losse of their liues.

71 *Item,* no man in their marching through what place soeuer they shall passe, shall set any thing on fire, as not their cabbins and incamped place at their departing, without commandement from the chiefe Generall, vpon the paine of the losse of their liues.

72 *Item,* if at any time, any man shall in the time of his drunkenesse quarrell and fight with his fellow, and in so doing, chance to kill him, he shall in so doing receiue as great punishment by death, as if he had beene sober.

73 *Item,*

73 *Item*, if any fouldier doe drinke himfelfe drunke, or be found drunke, within the compaffe of the day and night of his watch and fpecially if he be vnable to ftand in Sentinell, or doe his dutie, fuch a one muft be moft fe-uerely punifhed.

74 *Item*, note that fouldiers fhall fweare at their firft entring into feruice that they will faithfully and truely ferue their Captaine for fix monthes together, and when the fix monthes are expired, they fhall fweare to ferue .him fix monthes more, if he need them : And if the Captaine needeth them not fo long, but mindes to dif-charge his band, the Captaine fhall allow each of them halfe a monthes wages at his departing, and fo difcharge them.

75 *Item*, there fhall no man make any fhout, or other ftirring noife in any corner or open place of citie, towne, caftle, fort or campe, whereby any danger or inconue-nience may grow vnto the company any manner of waies, on paine of the loffe of his life.

76 *Item*, he that fhall difclofe the watch-word to ene-mie or friends, except it be to fuch a one as he fhall bee appointed by his Gouernour : or fhall be found a fleepe in the watch, fcout, or ward, fhall be punifhed with death.

77 *Item*, if any Captaine for corruption fake, fhall giue licence to his owne fouldier, or to any other foul-dier without the licence of the Generall to depart the campe, fhall receiue the fame punifhment that the foul-dier fhould receiue.

78 *Item*, that no fouldier fhould go out of the campe in the night time without the watch-word, in danger of his life, for if he be flaine fo by the watch, there is no blame to be laid vpon them that kill him.

79 *Item*, there fhall no fouldier go out of the campe without his armour and other weapons vpon the paine of the loffe of his life.

80 *Item*, euery captaine fhall be fworne, that he fhall charge euery Corporall vpon his oath, that hee fhall denounce euery Souldier that is vnder his charge, and that is not able and meete to ferue.

81 *Item*, in like cafe if the faid Corporall fhall receiue any new or ftrange fouldier into his band, his part and dutie is, that he giue vnto the higher Captaine knowledge thereof.

82 *Item*, no man of what condition foeuer he be, fhall be fo bold as to conuey away any Offendor vpon the paine of the loffe of his life.

83 *Item*, that euery fouldier fhall haue vpon his vttermoft garment fome fpeciall figne or token, whereby he may be knowne, fuch a one as the higher Captaines fhall agree vpon. As for example, he fhall haue vpon his garment a red-croffe, and vpon his armour a red-lace or fuch like, whereby he may the better be knowne of his fellowes: and if there be any fhall be found without the faid fignes and tokens, he fhall be vfed as an Aduerfary, or enemy.

84 *Item*, that all fouldiers, entring into battaile, affault, skirmifh, or other faction of armes, fhall haue for their common crie and word *S. George*, *S. George*, forward or vpon them, *S. George*, whereby the fouldier is much comforted, and the enemie difmaide, by calling to minde the auncient valour of *England*, which with that name hath beene fo often victorious, and therefore he that fhall malicioufly omit it fhall be feuerely punifhed for his obftinacie.

K

85 *Item*, if any Captaine or other Officers ſhall procure skirmiſh, or fight the battaile without commandment from the higher Officers, for ſo offending, they ſhall receiue death.

86 *Item*, if that any number of ſouldiers be commanded, and placed by the head Captaines, to defend or keep any citie, tower, caſtle or fort, or any other place, and they being ſharpely aſſaulted by the enemie, once, twice, or thrice, or oftner, in this caſe the law of Armes is, that the Lord Generall ſhall allow, and pay vnto ſuch a number of Souldiers but ordinarie wages: neither is there by law of armes any thing more due vnto them: And if the ſaid caſtles, towers, or fortreſſe, ſhall be ſold or be betraied by the ſaid Captaine, Officers, or ſouldiers, or otherwiſe yeelded, without the commandment of the Prince, or at the appointment of the Generall: ſhall be as falſe Traitors vſed.

87 *Item*, if any Captaine, Lieutenant, Sergeant, Corporall, or other Officer, or ſouldiers, giue into the hands of the enemie, any citie, fortreſſe, tower, or place of defence, doth incurre, as I haue ſaid, the danger of death, if he by chance be not more then conſtrained to deliuer vp the ſame, or that it is like a man of valour would haue done ſo: and therefore they ought neuer to abandon the place, for words or letters of the enemie, neither at the ſight of the inuironing campe: for it is not lawfull for the Caſtellane to leaue his Caſtle, if he haue victuals, men, and munition, or doth hope for ſuccours. Therefore reſpect is to be had, which muſt be holden as a Maxime, that where the place may be defended by aſſault without batterie, that at leaſt one aſſault is to be abidden, and mo to be aſpected if it be poſſible: and if it

can

can fuffer batterie, they muft abide at the leaft a volee of Canons: and if the place be fo weake that it cannot fuftaine, neither the one nor the other, and that it be farre diftant from fuccours: to yeeld doth merit neither punifhment of the Prince, nor of the enemie: but otherwife being of force, able to fuftaine rhe enemies furie, and cowardly or traiteroufly to deliuer the fame, merites death of the one and the other.

88 *Item*, if there be any citie, caftle or other fort, yeelded vp by the enemie, without expugnation: there fhall no man be fo bold to enter into the faid place, to fpoile or otherwife to kill or doe any outrage, without leaue of the Generall, vpon paine of the loffe of his life.

89 *Item*, there fhall no man depart out from the precinct of the campe, with any bootie or fpoile, without leaue of the chiefeft Officers or head Captaine, vpon the paine of the loffe of his life.

90 *Item*, if any man for feare forfaketh the place appointed him to fight in, and for feare throweth downe his weapon, the Officers or *Souldiers* may kill him without any danger.

91 *Item*, if any man faying that he hath done fome wrothy thing in fight, and it be proued contrary, hee fhall be punifhed.

92 *Item*, if a Regiment, or Band, fhall by mutinies or otherwife incurre the lawes of the field, it is requifite and neceffary, for that all fhall not be put to death, that euery mans name be taken and put into a bagge, and that the tenth Lot fhould be executed: The which although euery man doe not feele, yet neuertheleffe he fhall feare the euent.

93 *Item*, at fuch times as the Generall or Captaine

doth

doth mufter, traine, or faine any battaile, skirmifh, affault, or other warlike encounter, if any fouldier doth
either negligently or wittingly, hurt, maime, or kill his
companion with pouder, bullet, or by what meanes foeuer, fuch a one fhall feuerely, and exemplarly be punifhed accordingly.

94 *Item*, that each Corporall, and other Officer,
fhall haue either in written hand or print, thefe Martiall
lawes, and this booke, wherein a priuate Souldier is inftructed, bought and prouided at the charges of the
whole fquadron out of their pay, to the end that it being
continually repeated to the Souldiers, no man may plead
ignorance, but receiue condigne punifhment according
to his offence.

95 *Item*, that euery Captaine, Lieutenant, Enfigne-
bearer, Sergeant or Corporall, fo often as their bands,
fquadrons, and fouldiers enter into ward, fhall appoint
the Clarke of the band or fome one that can read, once
in the day or in the night, to read vnto the company
(that muft attentiuely giue eare) not onely thefe Martiall
lawes here fet downe, but alfo all the courfe of thefe
directions belonging to a priuate fouldier, Corporall,&c.
contained in this booke, for their inftructions, vnder
paine of open punifhment by the Generall, or Marfhall.

96 *Item*, that the forefaid Officers after one twelue
monthes feruice, wherein the fouldier hath had fufficient
experience, and is inured in thefe precepts and directions,
they fhall euen as the Schoole-mafter doth the children,
call euery one particularly to account, and examine
them feuerely herein, and to efteeme thofe for old and
perfect fouldiers, that know thefe lawes and their dutie
by heart, and at their fingers ends, and the reft Bifonians
                                                                      and

and freſh water-ſouldiers, that are ignorant, although they haue ſerued ſeuen yeares, yea and to place them in the moſt ſeruile ſeruices. And if there be any that maliciouſly or diſdainfully perſiſt in their blunt ignorance, either to diſarme them, and diſcharge them, or elſe to puniſh them with open ſhame and infamie.

97 *Item*, if there be any man that ſhall infring, and not maintaine, confirme, and to his power diligently and dutifully keepe and obſerue theſe articles aforeſaid, ſuch ſhall as periured perſons with all ſeueritie be puniſhed : And if any ſouldier or ſouldiers ſhall offend in any manner of thing that doth belong and appertaine to the dutie of a ſouldier, whereof there is no mention made in theſe articles, ſuch an Offender ſhall be puniſhed at the diſcretion of the Marſhall of the field and Generall.

Theſe articles muſt be openly read in the preſence of the chiefe Captaines , by the Notary or Scribe of the Court, and after that they be read, the Oath ſhall be miniſtred vnto euery man by the Pretor in this wiſe , or the like words, to the ſame end and purpoſe : ſpeaking vnto the whole company, and ſaying ; my brethren and friends, that are heere preſent, you haue heard the articles of our Soueraigne, containing the chiefe and principall points of our rights and lawes of the fielde , and of the Oath, and the manner thereof, which euery Souldier ought to take. All you that doe meane faithfully and valiantly to obſerue, maintaine, fulfill, confirme , and keepe the foreſaid Articles, let him heere now either openly refuſe to be a Souldier , or with mee hold vp his finger, and ſay after me.

All theſe Articles which haue beene openly red vnto vs, we hold and allow as ſacred and good, and thoſe will

we

wee truely and ftoutly confirme, fulfill, maintaine, and keepe fo helpe vs G O D, and his diuine word, *Amen*.

Thefe Articles with others, which for tedioufneffe I omit, would be publifhed, fome vpon paine of death, fome with greater, and fome with leffe punifhment, to euery one that doth offend, without any remiffion or forgiueneffe, or regard of bloud, degree, kindred, or friendfhip : fpecially at the beginning to lie in campe, whereby the armie may the better be fet in good order, and to make it fearefull of God, of iuftice, and of the Generall, with loue and feare.

The execution hereof only appertaineth to the mafter of the Campe, for the hearing, ordering, and determining of the caufes of iuftice vnder the Generall, as the Lieutenant of a city or towne, Deputie for the Prince. For the mafter of the campe is the chiefe of the orders, who hath place in the fielde in many things as principall next to the Generall who hath the chiefe gouernment in pitching the campe, and diflodging.

Briefly from the Generall downward, it is the greateft charge and burden that is in the armie, and therefore it is requifite that hee haue good knowledge and remembrance of all the Orders whereby the warres is to be gouerned, and that he be of good practife and experience, and duely obeyed.

But fuch cafes as are capitall and of great importance, fhould be heard and determined by the Generall and his Iudges : It fufficeth that God is the knower and determiner, of all things, and next vnto him his Deputies vpon earth : who failing to doe iuftice, either for loue, or hatred, fhall yeelde account thereof before the diuine

uine Iudge, and this law cannot be auoided by vs, but we shall be cited and called without appeale.

Chap. VI.

Briefe Notes of other meane offices, as Drummes, Fifes, Surgeons, and the Clarke of the Band.

DRummes and Fifes muſt be choſen of able qualities and perſonage, ſecret and ingenious, skilfull in the ſound and vſing of their inſtruments, which muſt warne as the mouth of a man to all intents of ſeruice, diligent in times conuenient to inſtruct Souldiers in the ſame, that none by ignorance neglect their duties. Theſe be often-times ſent on meſſages, importing charge, which of ne-ceſſitie require languages, ſomtimes to ſummon or com-mand the enemies to render, ſometimes carie ranſomes, or redeeme, or conduct Priſoners. Many other things to them doe appertaine, as before is rehearſed &c.

A Chyrurgion is neceſſarie to be had in euery band, who ought to be an honeſt man, ſober, and of good counſell, skill in his ſcience, able to heale and cure all kind of ſores, wounds, and griefes: to take a bullet out of the fleſh and bone, and to ſlake the fire of the ſame, and that he haue all his tooles and inſtruments with other neceſ-ſary ſtuffe, as oyles, balmes, ſalues, ſtepres, roulers, bol-ſters, ſplenters, and all other things to the ſcience belong-ing, which alſo ought to haue courage for his patient, and allowed ſtuffe, he ſhall readily imploy his induſtrie vpon the ſore and wounded, and not intermedling with others, to his owne charge noiſome. Such be placed with the

Enſigne,

Enſigne, and lodged neere to the Captaine, and neere their baldrickes in time of fight, which by law of the field is their. charter.

The Clarke of a band would be a man choſen of a diſcreete behauiour, ſuch a one as hath the vſe of his penne and skilfull in Arithmetike, who muſt haue a booke in the which he muſt write all the names of the Souldiers appertaining to the band, diuiding euery weapon by themſelues, that they may be the readier to be muſtred, and otherwiſe to be placed in order of march, at watch and ward the clarke muſt be attentiue with his booke, to call uery mans name, to ſee who is abſent, and that certificate thereof be made vnto the Captaine, who muſt as before is rehearſed, without ſickneſſe or ſome licence of the head Officers ſee him or them puniſhed to the example of all others. He muſt ſon: ·nes in the watch and ward read vnto the ſouldiers, the Military lawes and directions, cauſing firſt a ſolemne ſilence to be made, and then proceed in reading, examining, and conferring with euery particular and common ſouldier, touching his memorie of theſe things, for his full inſtruction. Alſo the Clarke is to take charge of the Captaines munition, who ſeeing it deliuered vnto the ſouldiers, muſt take note how much is deliuered, vnto whom, and what day of the moneth it is deliuered, with the priſe. Likewiſe he muſt repaire to the Clarke of the victuals, and by the Captaines warrant receiue ſuch bread, beere and other victuals, as is to be had, and to deliuer it to thoſe that ſhall be thought by the Captaine to be of credit, to victuall the band by the Princes price, and to take tickets of them as well for that it is deliuered vnto them, as what they doe deliuer vnto ſouldiers. Alſo he muſt in the Captaines name and

by

by his warrant repaire vnto the Merchants and other A r
tificers, and take such wares as the Officers and souldiers
haue need of, who must at the pay day by the Captaine
be answered. Also prouided that the Victualler alloweth
but the Souldier six-pence a day, the ouerplus goeth to
their paiment of furniture and apparell.

The Clarke must oft peruse the tickets to see that no
more be deliuered then their wages come to, that the
Captaines thereby receiue no losse. The Clarke ought to
inquire when any be departed this world, also when any
be slaine, and discharged the band, and to make a iust
note thereof, whereby certificate may be made to the
Muster-master, that the Prince in no waies may be hin-
dered, neither the Captaines by the Victuallers receiue
any detriment or losse. Finally, he must vpon the report
of the Corporals or other Officers, finde and procure of
the Captaines, reliefe for the sicke, and wounded Souldiers and Prisoners, which ought to be redeemed out of
the enemies hand.

CHAP. VII.
The Prelates charge that takes care of SOVLDIERS *of the* BAND.

TO knit vp this first discourse of Militarie Directions, and Martiall lawes, speciall care must be had to
prouide one man amongst the many scores of Souldiers,
that may gouerne and direct in spirituall causes, who
ought to be wise, learned, honest, sober, patient, and of
exemplar life : who must offer vp daily praiers for his
L   whole

whole companie, muſt inſtruct them to be penitent and to reſtore to euery man his right : to communicate in Catholike and Chriſtian manner , ſo often as they can, chiefly at ſpeciall times appointed by the Church,and before any dangerous attempt, to feede them with holeſome foode of learned inſtructions, wherein they may learne how to liue, and ſo conſequently to teach their companies their duties towards God and their Prince, and to giue ghoſtly counſell and ſpirituall reliefe vnto the ſicke wounded, weake in body or in conſcience, and that ſuch be well armed with ſpirituall armour , that is , with good knowledge and good liuing , ready to perſwade them manfully to withſtand their enemies , the fleſh, the deuill, the world and deſperation , putting them in ſure hope through the equitie of their cauſe , their conformitie to the Church, and their firme faith in our Sauiour Ieſus Chriſt , to enter into the campe of euerlaſting life, where they ſhall ride amongſt the Souldiers on white Horſes, clothed in white and pure ſilke , crowned with bright triumphant garlands, as the Scriptures doe witnes. This and ſuch like belongs vnto ſuch perſonages as take care of the ſouldiers in a warlike band.

Now then to conclude , and to make an end of my firſt diſcourſe, I would wiſh all valiant minded ſouldiers, carefully to carrie in minde thoſe precepts which are proper and due vnto a priuate Souldier, which I partly haue collected and ſet downe in this ſhort pamphlet, that when he ſhall be called vnto an hier office, he may deſeruedly aſcend the third ſtep of Martiall office, and ſo by degrees riſe to the height of ſupreame gouernment.

CHAP. VIII.

Chap. VIII.

How Pikes are to be carried in aray, march or battaile.

THose that are appointed to carie Pikes in aray of rankes or baite l, muſt know that Pikes amongſt all other weapons that belongs to Souldiers, is of greateſt honour and credite : and truely, whoſoeuer doth carie and manage the ſame weapon well and with good grace, doth make a very beautifull and pleaſant ſhew to the Beholders, and chiefly when it is caried vpon the ſhoulder, ſuſtained and ſupported with a good grace, and the hand that doth ſuſtaine it be on that ſide the ſhoulder where it is placed, and with *il Gombedo alto.*

They muſt likewiſe be aduertiſed which march in the formoſt rankes, if they be vpon the right ſide, to hold their Pikes continually in marching in the right hand, and vpon the right ſhoulder without euer changing it : and ſo likewiſe being vpon the left ſide of the ranke, to hold it alwaies vpon the left ſhoulder : thoſe that be in the midſt of the rankes haue libertie to vſe that ſide that is beſt for their commoditie, either vpon the right or left hand, and to moue their Pikes from ſhoulder to ſhoulder at their choiſe and pleaſure : It is true that the iuſt carying of the Pike of thoſe that march in the midſt of the rankes, is to hold it vpon the left ſhoulder, and to carie their right hand behind vpon their dagger, or vpon their ſide, and ſo generally all, as well they that be in the midſt, as thoſe that be in the head of the rankes are to obſerue this or-

L 2   der,

der, to carie that hand which is at libertie behinde them, or vpon their fides. Let him march then with a good grace, holding vp his head gallantly, his pace full of grauitie and ftate, and fuch as is fit for his perfon, and let his body bee ftraight and as much vpright as is poffible, and that which moft imports, is that they haue alwaies their eies vpon their compan ons which are in ranke with them, and before them going iuft one with the other, and keeping perfit diftance without committing error in the leaft pace or ftep, and euery pace and motion with one accord and confent, they ought to make at one inftant time. And in this fort all the rankes entirely are to go, fometimes foftly, fomtimes faft, according to the ftroke of the drumme. The heele and tippe of their pikes would bee equally holden, both of length and height, as neere as is poffible, to auoide that they fall not out to be by bearmg them otherwife, like vnto organ-pipes, fome long, fome fhort. The meafure and proportion thereof, to hold the heele of the Pike is this : It is neceffarie for him to haue an eye to the ranke that doth march before him, and fo carie the Butt-end or heele of his pike, that it may bee iuft ouer againft the ioynt of the hamme of the fouldier, that in march fhall be ftraight before him : and fo euery one from hand to hand muft obferue the proportion of that height, that is right behind vpon the ioynt of the knee, for by doing fo they cannot commit error, carying in their march that legge that is vnder that arme that fuftaines and caries the Pike of iuft and euen proportion, by mouing their pace right vnder the ftaffe of the Pike, going in their march, as I haue faid before, iuft and

euen

euen, with a gallant and ſtately, and ſumptuous paçe :
for by doing ſo, they ſhall be eſteemed, honoured,
and commended of the Lookers on, who
ſhall take wonderfull delight to behold them march in that
order.

L 3 THE

THE
SECOND BOOKE
OF MILITARY
Directions:

Wherein is set downe the office of a Ser-
geant, Ensigne-bearer, Lieutenant, the
Gentlemen of a band, and how to skirmish, and discouer.

Chap. I.

And first, the Office of the Sergeant of a Band.

Ince euery Officer through his con-
tinuall exercise and daily diligence
in executing his charge, doth attaine vnto perfit experience by daily practise, which is as it were con-
uerted into nature: therefore hee
which determines with himselfe to
be accounted sufficient and of abi-
litie, to discharge the place of a good Sergeant of a band,
with a forward intent to learne and be thorowly instruct-
ed, ought first to be a Souldier that hath seene much,
and

and a Corporall of good experience, according to the directions of my first booke: In which two roomes it is very conuenient, that he haue tasted and beene present at great diuersitie of seruice, and warlike enterprises, and to carie a resolute minde to delight in the exercise of this office, to the end he be not found therein irresolute and ignorant: and that likewise he faile not in the ready performing of any enterprise, when Martiall affaires do call him forth to put the same in execution.

First of all it is very requisite that he haue most perfitly in memorie, the number of all the souldiers of the band, and distinctly with what weapons they are armed, what quantity of Corslets and Pikes, how many armed and disarmed carie short weapons, what number of Hargabusiers with murrians and without, how many musketeares, how many light armed pikes and targets of proofe, that the better and more readily vpon a sodaine, hee may put the company in order

He must euer plant the best armed in places most necessarie, as at the front and backe, the right and left side of a square. The first ranke in ordinarie long marching, the targets of proofe must go in as a ready couer and bulwarke against the enemies shot: next to them the musketeares, then the Hargabusiers, and after them the armed and light pikes: amidst whose rankes he must at all times place the Ensigne, garded with Halberds or bils, and then againe the light armed and armed pikes, hargabuse and musket-eares, and last of all targets of proofe: by this equality of diuision, the whole band at one instant shall be ready to receiue any suddaine surprise of the enemie. The Sergeant carrying these things in his minde, hauing laid a distinct plat, he may very easily vary their
forme

forme and order as he shall be appointed, and as the situation of the place doth require, or the accidents of warre doe constraine.

He must neuer worke vnwarily, or at all aduentures, and tending to no determined purpose, as those that doe not remember the perfit rules and reckonings of their office, whereof there be now adaies ouer many, for when it is necessary for them to alter their order, and that perforce they must quite change the forme and fashion that then they obserue, they know not which way to beginne. Therefore to the end his order and rankes may be to the purpose duely and directly changed, and with facilitie disposed: let him euer disseuer and diuide one part of his weapons from an other, causing euery one to turne and enter into their rankes and order by themselues, so shall hee proceed in taking away, setting forward, and intermixing one sort of rankes within another very orderly. And thereby the full proportion of his band shall be framed, as he hath determined, or as it is deuised by him that commands, either in marching forward and backward, or in turning without disorder, by 3. 5. 7. or 9. in a ranke, as the Lieutenant, Captaine, or Sergeant maior appoints.

He ought euer to beware that in ordering the rankes, and appointing the souldiers their places, that they begin not to make debate, or stomacke one another for dignitie of place; the which doth oftentimes fall out to their great annoy and damage, and the Officers tedious toile: For in enterprises of great importance, euen in the presence of the invading enemy, some vaine-glorious fellowes are accustomed to striue for the chiefest places: the which roomes by all reason, and of dutie appertaine

to

to the beſt armed, and not to any others, whoſe vnruly
raſhnes may be the ruine of the whole band. Therefore
fit and conuenient places are to be obſerued with humilitie, the naked in their places, and the armed in theirs:
But to touch one point, which we haue already ſpoken
of, I iudge it moſt conuenient that the armed (thoſe for
skirmiſh excepted) muſt remaine in maine ſtands and
battailes, as ſome ſay, to abide by the ſtake, who ought to
be ſo well armed, as they may beare and ſupport the
blowes of their enemies, and reſiſt any furious charge, either of horſemen or footmen: whereas beſide their well
ordered ranks, by reaſon they be armed, they make a
more gallant ſhow; giuing courage to thy owne people,
and diſcourage to the enemie, and in proofe are more
profitable than the diſarmed, who remaining in their
roomes, the contrary ſucceeds.

The Sargeant of the Company muſt haue ſpeciall regard when victuals cannot be had for money, by forrage
or otherwiſe, to make repaire togither with the Clarke of
the Band, to the principall munitions, that his company
taſte not of famine; and from thence procure to haue ſo
much as he well can, or as is conuenient, and according
to his receiued order, ſo muſt he depart and diſtribute all
manner of munitions amongſt the Corporals, that euery
one of them may giue to their ſoldiers their portions.

The like ought he to vſe, touching powder for the
Harquebuſiers and musketiers, lead for bullets, match
for them to burne, and ech thing elſe whereof they haue
neede, to the end they may alwaies remaine in order,
and be very well prouided and ſtored, as neere as is poſſible, and as is moſt conuenient; and to perſwade the ſoldier that to gaine a place of more account, he will ſpare

M   his

his pay to arme himfelfe the more brauely. He muft likewife haue diligent eye, that the faid munition of match and powder be conferued warily from wetting, and kept with a fpeciall fpare from vntimely fpending: for this prouident precept doth import very much in all enterprifes, by reafon that the negligence of the Sargeant, touching this neceffarie fore-fight and care, hath bin the caufe that the fhot haue not bin able readily to performe their duties according to the appointed determinations, or as neceffitie did require, by reafon of their vnwary keeping their munition in wet weather, or their generall want through vaine mifpence, by which meanes many and moft notable errors haue fucceeded of great loffe & moment, and to the hinderance, fhame, and totall ruine of a whole company or campe.

Therefore it is moft expedient that the Sargeant, togither with the feuerall Corporals, do diligently and narrowly examine, vifit, fearch, and view the proper flaskes, tuch-boxes, pockets, and other places where the foldiers are accuftomed to carry and keepe their powder and match, and perufe diligently all thofe things without negligence, fayning, or fauouring: diuers haue receiued great ignominie and fhame in their office, for want of the performance thereof: whereas by carrying a contrary care, they haue bin vniuerfally well thought of, and commended of all good foldiers and valiant Captaines. Therefore as occafion doth ferue and offer, he may admonifh, put in minde, and reprehend with dexteritie the foldiers vnder his charge and guiding. To him it appertaines to lay his helping hands about all things neceffarie for his company, as well in prouiding for them, as difpencing, or deferring neceffary charges, except for the prouifion

uifion and diuiding of lodgings, which is the office of the Furrier or Harbinger, who ought to be very tractable, diligent, and altogether officious, not being partiall to any one for peculiar profit or pleafure, and therefore it is neceffary a Sargeant fhould know how to write, for it is hard by memory to difcharge his charge.

The Sargeant muft be carefull to accompanie, at the houre appointed, the guard to the place of the watch, in going vp and downe alongft their flanks when he hath placed them in order, to fee them keepe due diftance, make the Laumband, march in ftraight line with their ranks, carry their armes in conformable proportion; and if vpon pleafure they giue a volee of fhot in paffing, to aduertife them to doe it orderly with due forme, one ranke after another, as they paffe ouer againft the Generall, or other great officer or perfonage and not in a confufed fort altogither, or by peeces. When he is arriued at the Corps of guard, and hath placed euery one in order, and prouided for all things neceffarie for the watch of that night, he muft then giue his aduife and counfell to the Corporalls, that they keepe good order in their Sentinels; yea fometimes and very often, it is good that he himfelfe aide them to chofe out the moft fit places for them to ftand in, to the end that the circuit of ground, which for all their fafeties is to be kept, may be conueniently guarded.

At the ioyning of the day and the night, or fomwhat later, he fhall fecretly giue the Corporalls the watchword, with the which they are to gouerne the guard as well by night as day : the which word by the commandment of his Captaine, hee muft procure the *Sargeant maior* to giue him, or of fome other that fhall haue the

charge

charge to giue the fame for want of his prefence, or in place of this great officer.

He muft arme himfelfe in fuch fort, that he be no leffe apt than any other foldier to be able at time of neede, both to defend himfelfe, and offend the enemie: touching which effect, Duke *Octauio Farnefe* in the expedition of 12000 footmen, and 600 horfemen, which *Paul* the third, Pope of Rome, fent into Germanie againft the Religion, did difpofe that all the Sargeants of his bands fhould arme themfelues with Harquebufes and murrians ; faying, that fo great a number of valiant men being Sargeants, as was in fo great an affembly and expedition of fuch importance, it was neither good nor commendable, that they fhould onely be armed with their Halberds, and therefore he ought to haue his page or Muchacho fecond him with thofe furnitures : neither feems it inconuenient, but hauing placed in order all things pertaining to his office, that he place himfelfe in ranke with the reft of the foldiers, yet in fuch a place as he may eafily depart from thence when neceffitie cals him away, to reforme or vfe remedie to any diforder he vnderftands of.

He muft with dexteritie proceed in reprehending and exhorting the foldiers to keep their due order, and not to difband and ftray abroad, but vpon needfull and lawfull occafions, and to take order in all other particular points, which are requifite to be obferued for the honor and profit of the Company, which things are chiefly to be procured and obferued by other officers.

Let him beware and abftaine from beating of foldiers at any time, that thereby he grow not odious : for it is not conuenient nor comely for an officer to ftrike a foldier,

dier, for thereby he fo offends, that he doth incurre the
paine to receiue punifhment for fo doing, of his Captaine
or the Mafter of the Campe.

He muft be diligent, carefull, and vigilant in all his affaires; for in this office, diligence and dexteritie is both
to the purpofe and moft neceffarie.

It is neceffarie he be alwaies conformable vnto the
Sargeant maior, by imitation and obedience in action, and
like his fhadow, to fecond him in all his doings; of
whom he may alwaies receiue information and order of
all fuch things as be neceffarie for feruice of his band:
and of him he may learne to proceed by conformitie, in
that which is conuenient for his office. For he that is in
company with men of vertue and valour, that be of more
excellent qualitie than he himfelfe, fhall euer reape fome
profit; and the rather for that he is bound to be in the
fight, and neere about the *Sargeant maior*, at all fuch
times as any thing is to be done, where he ought with a
good eare, and diligent eye, giue ready attendance, to
execute fuch commiffion as fhall be giuen him; efpecially thofe which appertaines to the ordering of the
rankes, and euery thing elfe whatfoeuer, without doing
any thing vpon his owne iudgment, but conferre with
that great officer, towards whom he muft alwaies be
courteous and conformable; and with an obedient and
beneuolent minde diligently imitate him.

I fuppofe it moreouer neceffarie, as I faid before, that
he be able to write and read, confidering the infinite
number of things which are to paffe through his hands,
and which he ought to execute for the benefit of his
company, which cannot be alwaies ordered, difpofed,
and guided only by memory: So confequently the Sar-

M 3   geant

geant is to take diligent heed and care of all the forefaid things to execute the points of his office fpeedily, and to rebuke and teach fuch as do amiffe with lenitie; and although he cannot violently ftrike and hurt any man, yet neuerthelesse no man can refift his authoritie, but obferue the fame as to the Captaines owne perfon, if he were prefent.

He is not to heare any mutinous or rebellious words amongft the company, but immediatly to reueale the fame, that fpeedy reformation may be had, and faults amended. And thus muft he be ftill occupied to reform mens manners, mifpence of munition, broken araies, and to be ready day and night to feruice, by the Captaine or Lieutenants commandment, and to inftruct the Company, to march, traine, and trauaile, as well by fignes from him framed, as otherwife by words fpoken, and to haue fpeciall regard to the company, to fee that their armour and weapons be in a readineffe alwaies for feruice: for the diligent and skilfull vfage of this office, is of no fmall moment to any good order throughout the whole band; no leffe than the Centurion amongft the Romanes, who was Captaine ouer a hundreth; and fo likewife euery hundreth in each band ought to haue a feuerall Sargeant to direct and gouerne.

Chap. II.
The Office of an Alfierus or Enfigne-bearer.

IF it be a thing moft requifite that a priuate foldier fhould haue a fpeciall zeale ouer his proper honor and credit; how much more is the fame neceffarie for a valiant

liant *Alfierus* or Enſigne-bearer. Therefore he muſt with
all carefull diligence, due diſcretion, aſcend the 4ᵗʰ degree
of this honorable diſcipline, being already trained vp in
the three firſt degrees, which is, of a priuate ſoldier, a
Corporall, and a Sargeant, whereby to his great commendation he may ſufficiently merit the ſway of this office.

Hauing ſolemnly receiued the Enſigne of his Captaine, like a noble and expert ſoldier, he ought carefully
to keepe the ſame, and beare a certaine reuerent reſpect
to it, as to a holy thing, yea & to be iealous ouer the ſafetie thereof, no leſſe than an amorous perſon ouer his louing miſtreſſe: ſince that onely with the ſacred ſhade of
the Enſigne, being well guided, the generall reputation
of all the band and company is conſerued.

Therefore the *Alfierus* ought to be endowed with
ſuch cuſtome, and vſe himſelfe with ſuch curteſie and ci-
uilitie, that he may not only procure the loue of his con-
federates, and friends, but of all the entire company.

Beſides, it is neceſſarie to haue neere vnto him a couple
of aſſiſtants at the leaſt, that be practiſed and good ſoldiers, which may be of the number of the Halberdiers
that go next his Enſigne, to the end that when he is conſtrained to abſent himſelfe from the ſame, through ſome
vrgent and neceſſarie occaſion (for otherwiſe it is not to
be permitted) he may cauſe one of them take care and
charge of his Enſigne, in what accident ſoeuer might
fall out during that time : for that thing ought neuer to
be left alone or abandoned to a ſlender and looſe guard,
which is of ſuch a great importance, whereupon euery
mans honor and eſtimation dependeth ; wherefore it
ought of all to be carefully kept, and well accompanied.

Note that the *Alfierus*, to defend his Enſigne and himſelfe

felfe at one inftant, muft haue in his one hand his drawne
fword, and in the other the Enfigne : which thing is
conuenient of him particularly to be performed, when it
is time to affault the enemies vpon a wall, Trench, Scalade, Bulwarke, Breach, or in any ftrait paffage or enterprife, fince that with the point of yron of the Enfigne
ftaffe fmall defence can be made, as well for the weaknes
of the ftaffe, as through the trouble and continuall waue-
ring of the filke which is about it, fo that in bearing the
fame difplayed he ought rather to haue regard where he
fhall fet his foote, than to the top of the ftaffe, or any
other place leffe neceffarie, as well thereby to flie affectation, which in carying thereof is made manifeft, as alfo to
conduct the fame with more affured courage.

Moreouer, note that the moft honorable place of the
threde or ranke is the right hand, and the fecond the left
hand ; which degrees likewife be obferued in all the
rankes of other foldiers, afwell as when diuers Enfignes
do march togither in one ranke : for amongft the bands
and fquares of foldiers, the flanks do alwaies refift the
affaults and furie of the enemie ; as the fides which be
neereft to them, be alwaies guarded of thofe that be moft
practifed, and the middle part not, only except the firft
and laft ranke of the ordinance or battaile, where the
middeft is the place of greateft eftimation ; for the head
or backe of the fquare being affaulted, they then withftand the greateft furie. And by good reafon, for this
place of the midft is euer much more broken and endo-
maged of the enemies armes and force, than any other
part : wherefore amongft expert and valiant foldiers,
this roome is of greateft honor, and of moft eftimation,
as the place that hath greateft neede of defence, which
being

being fubiect to more open and manifeft perill than the reft be, is of greateft dignitie. For Captaines are accufto-med to fhew notable and fingular fauor to that foldier, which they prefer to an enterprife of perill and danger, fo that it be capable of iffue and altogither defperate.

Neither is this to be accounted for a maruell; for as this profeffion is altogither different from others,fo like-wife the orders, and ceremonies are diuerfly managed, if a man may terme thofe things ceremonies,which of ne-ceffitie ought with diligence to be gouerned with great care,arte,and induftry:It behoues the *Alfierus*,whileft he doth march in ordinance amidft the band,to go with a graue and ftately pace, aduifedly and couragioufly ioy-ned with modeftie, and without affectation or vaine bra-uery : neither ought he to bow or decline his body at any time to any perfon, that thereby he may reprefent and maintaine the reputation and excellencie of armes, and the Enfigne before his Prince, chiefe Ruler, Lord Gene-rall,Coronell,Captaine,Gouernor &c. As he paffeth be-fore them,he ought to abafe the points and tip of the En-figne, or rather with his arme bow downe neere-hand all the ftaffe of the Enfigne, and fo much more, by how much he is of greater dignitie and authoritie. In this fort fhall he make figne of reuerence,and not pull off his cap or hat, neither bend his knee, nor moue any one part of his perfon, thereby to retaine that dignitie due to the Enfigne and his office.

The *Alfierus* being in fquare, ranke,or ordinance, with the Enfigne difplaid, doth change (almoft neuer) the place where he is planted to march, which is in the midft of the footmen, as a place moft fafe and beft defended. Therefore thofe that otherwife would vfe it, do ground

N   their

their opinion vpon fome ancient order of the Romanes or Grecians, wherein they are deceiued, becaufe at this day we are conftrained to varie our order, confidering our armes be varied, which do now fetch and wound much more and further of, and are more piercing than thofe of ancient time.

Neither is it expedient to put this officer, which is of fuch great refpect, alwaies in hazard, as well for the good qualitie of his perfon, the which we muft alwaies prefuppofe him to be of, as alfo for the office of great importance he fupplies, fince he doth fuftaine the difplaid Enfigne, wherein the reputation and honor of all the company confifts. But at fuch time as he fhall march to a Scalade, breach and battery, the valiant *Alfierus* with his Enfigne in one hand, and his fword in another, as is before faid, ought to enforce himfelfe to be the firft, and by all meanes to mount vp, to enter amongft the enemies, and to aduance and inuite the reft forward, both his inferiors, companions, and betters: for in effect at fuch times the particular guiding of the band appertaines to him. Now to the intent that the foldiers at the inftant time of a dangerous enterprife, and in a comberfome and perillous time and place, may be inuited, and feruently ftirred vp to follow the Enfigne: He muft therefore vfe fuch curtefie to all men, that in all hazards and great exploits, he being beloued of the foldiers, may be very much aided and defended by them; whereas otherwife they do either fuffer open ignominie, or danger of death, when as they be either abandoned at the point of extremitie, or traiteroufly flaine or wounded by their owne companions and followers, as at the affault of *Dalahaui*, and a skirmifh of brauery at *Louaine*, chanced vnto two feuerall Enfignebearers

bearers of the Baron of *Sheueran*, Coronell ouer ten En-
figneś of fhot: therefore fince he is the fhadow of the
valour and good condition of his Captaine and companie,let him be carefull of his dutie.

The Enfigne-bearer may of his difcretion and authoritie, efpying the company trauaile,or follow enemies to
their difcommoditie and perill,loofing the winde, hill, or
ground of aduantage, difordering the aray,may ftand ftill,
and caufe the drums and fifes to ftand and found the retreat, that the company may refort and come to the Enfigne, and order the aray by the aduantage of the ground,
rather than abide the comming of the enemie.

He ought alwaies to haue about him, and to lodge
where he doth himfelfe, fo many good drums, as there
be hundreths in his band ; that at all times he may make
Raccolte, and gather his foldiers togither, and for fuch
like neceffarie refpects.

He ought neuer craue licence to go to any enterprife
whatfoeuer, for any defire he hath to make himfelfe
knowne, or to win fame, but ought to remaine ftedfaft
and firme, when his turne of feruice comes, in refpect of
the great charge he doth carry in the manage of the
Enfigne.

It is neceffarie to haue a horfe for his owne vfe, the
which whileft he marcheth ought to go neere the Enfigne,whether he be in fquare battaile or long march: for
by taking his eafe on horfebacke, he may keep himfelfe
continually luftie and frefh,and therewithall may accommodate his cariage, or baggage ; as fome foldiers may
likewife do among the ordinarie cariage, prouided for
by the Captaine.

Note that the Enfigne which he receiued of his Captaine,

taine, muſt by him be reſtored againe at ſuch times as he
is diſcharged out of the company ; if during the time of
his ſeruice, there hath not chanced a battaile, aſſault, or
other enterpriſe , wherein the *Alfierus* being preſent,
hath made manifeſt apparance, that he hath merited
and deſerued the ſame.   For in ſuch caſes it is to be vnderſtood, that he hath wonne and gained the ſame, and
not otherwiſe, vnleſſe the Captaine of his free will doth
giue it him, which is a very ancient cuſtome, eſpecially amongſt the Italians.

It is very requiſite the *Alfierus* haue beſides his two
Aſſiſtants, a valiant and couragious ſeruant, who is a practiſed ſoldier, and not a nouice, or yoongling, as ſome
very fondly and vnaduiſedly do entertaine now a-dayes,
that continually being neere him, as well in the maine
ſquare battaile, or elſewhere, to ſecond him with a peece,
pike, or target of proofe ; and may haue in ſuch a one
that entire faith and aſſured credit, that he ſhould haue of
a faithfull companion, whom he muſt not keepe, as an
abiect ſeruant, but he ought to maintaine him, apparell
him, and arme him with conuenient armes of deſence ;
for ſometimes it ſhall fall out in the day of a fought battaile of a whole armie, that thoſe deputed ſeruants may
haue the cuſtodie of all the Enſignes in the maine ſquare
battaile, and the *Alfierus* of ech company, as men wel armed bé placed in the head of the battaile, or in ſome o-
ther principall or neceſſarie places, which are to be gouerned and defended by practiſed and valiant ſoldiers ; as
particularly fell out at ſuch time as the *Marqueß* of *Vaſto*,
fought at *Creſola* in *Lombardie* againſt the Frenchmen,
which iourney was loſt by the Emperialiſts, although that
day they fought valiantly ; and beſides in other enterpriſes,

prifes, fuch men haue executed gallant feruice.

He muft alwaies prouide a fufficient *corps de guard* about his Enfigne, as well by day as night, in what place foeuer he fhall be, although no fufpicion were to be had of the enemie, that thereby he may remaine fafe from all fudden furprifes, or vnprouided cafualties, and the rather to maintaine the honor and reputation due to the Enfigne, whereby all finifter inconuenience may be auoyded, and the maieftie and office of the fame generally well refpected ; efpecially when time and place of fufpect minifters occafion. The *Alfierus* muft march to the guard, either armed with a Curafe of proofe, or fome other conuenient garment of defence, being ftill feconded with his feruant, who is to carry either target, halberd, peece, or pike, or fuch weapon as he doth delight in, which at the feat of the guard, taking his Enfigne in his hand, he muft let reft in the keeping of his feruant. Neither is it requifite in going or marching, that he vnlofe and difplay the Enfigne, without fome fpeciall occafion, but ought to referue the aduancing, and difplaying of the fame at full, vntill he come in the fight of the Cheiftaine or Prince, or in the fight of the enemie, or other places of feruice.

It is neceffarie his Enfigne haue certaine fpeciall counterfignes and markes, that it may eafily be knowne of his fouldiers, both neere hand and farre off, to the intent that in all exploits, and at vnknowne fuddaines, his fouldiers may perfitly perceiue the fame amongft the other Enfignes, different from the reft, wherein the Alfierus muft vfe an exquifite manage, that by his wife and valorous actions without any other mans relation , may be difcerned his vertuous actions and forward proceedings,

which

which he ought to make apparant by some notable enterprise.

The Alfierus must be a man of good account, of a good race, honest and vertuous, braue in apparell, thereby to honour his office, and continually armed as well when no perill is feared, as in time of danger, to giue example to the rest of the souldiers not to thinke their armour burthenous, but by vse to make it as familiar to him as his skinne. Finally, he must be a man skilfull, hardy, and couragious, of able courage to aduance and beare vp the Ensigne in all extremities, secret, silent, and zealous, able often to comfort, animate and encourage the company to take in hand, & maintaine such extremities, & enterprises, as they are appointed vnto, and neuer to retire, but when of noble policie, the higher Officers commaund the same. Vnto this Officer there should be certaine ceremonies vsed in deliuery of the Ensigne, receiuing it by oath in the presence of his band, at which time he must make vow and professe the same rather to be his winding sheete, and therein to lose his life, then through his default to lose the same : whereunto euery priuate souldier should likewise be sworne, as among the *Romanes* it was vsed, when he was not accounted a souldier, but a theefe, or robber, till hee had taken his oath. And therefore their warre was called *Militia Sacrata.*

CHAP. III.

CHAP. III.
The office of the Lieutenant of a Companie.

THat perſon vpon whom any charge doth depend, and doth deſeruedly manage any affaire, muſt frame himſelfe to vſe due diligence, and with dexteritie ſuffer ſuch tedious toile, as in theſe ſerious affaires ſucceed, ſince that charge (as I haue already ſaid) ſignifieth nothing elſe but a burthen of affaires.

Therefore that a ſouldier may deſeruedly mount vp to this degree of worthy honour and martiall dignitie, he muſt vſe all circumſpect care to performe his office like an expert Lieutenant, that the company be well gouerned, which he muſt accompliſh with a forward and willing minde (though of dutie hee is bound to performe the ſame) aſwell to content the minde of his Captaine, as to angment his owne honour and reputation. He muſt neuer appropriate vnto himſelfe any one point of authoritie, but diligently diſcipher and vnderſtand all things, and make relation thereof to his Captaine, of whom it is neceſſarie he take all his commiſſions and directions. His part is to giue willingly and readily counſell and aduiſe to his Captaine, as often as he is demanded, and otherwiſe neuer, vnleſſe he ſee that the ſame may doe manifeſt good, or in caſe of preſent perill.

The Lieutenant ought to carie with him a diligent care of concord, for that particularly the pacification of diſcords and difference amongſt the ſouldiers of his company, appertaines vnto him, which muſt be done without choler or paſſion, and muſt ſtill handle them very indifferently

rently and curteoufly. For his indifferencie, befides the
gaining of him truftie credite, doth make eafie the defci-
ding of any difference or difagreement, and is one point
which of neceffity is moft conuenient to an honourable
Peace-maker, although it be a very difficile thing to procure peace in points of honour, fpecially amongft fouldiers that ftand much vpon their punctos, and for that
refpect is it very hard to vfe a iuft balance. Therefore in
fuch cafes it is moft requifite that euery one of the in-
tereffed, fhew at the full his entire caufe, the which is a
thing not vulgar, neither of fmall importance. And although the Pacifier ought neuer to hang more vpon the
one fide then the other, yet it is conuenient he haue fome
fmall refpect to him that is wronged againft reafon, rather then to him that is the vnlawfull worker of the iniurie. But if he finde any difficultie in refoluing thefe dif-
ferences, let him conferre with the Captaine, to the end
that he, who is knowne to be the occafion, and will not
agree to an honeft end, may be immediately difcharged:
but if it be thought good that he remaine to ferue a time,
for the execution of fome fpeciall enterprife, then the
word both of the one and the other ought to be taken,
vntill the fame be performed or the pay paft, and then
may difcharge him, as is faid, to fhun a greater fcandale:
for to enter into vnquiet quarrelling and difcord, one e-
quall with an other, and with one that receiues the like
ftipend, is not the part and qualitie of a fubiect Souldier,
but of a free carelefle Cutter, and band-Buckler, and of
an infolent and importunate perfon, whofe nature doth
argue in him that his doings tend to an other end, then to
become excellent in the honourable exercife of armes.
Put the cafe that one of them fhould valiantly ouercome
the

the other, yet vnto the Captaine doth arife no other then
want, lofle, and euill fatisfaction : for when firft hee did
receiue them into his feruice, hee did prefume that they
were both of them equally to be efteemed, men of good
credite and behauiour, and that for fuch they were conducted and receiued ftipend. So that quarrelling and kil-
ling one the other, as often it falls out in refolute perfons,
or putting him to a difhonour or open foile : fuch a one
doth not onely depriue the Captaine of a Souldier, but
alfo of himfelfe likewife : for the law of reafon doth
binde the Captaine not to maintaine an importunate perfon, a malefactour, and an homicide, in one band no leffe
then a well ordered citie : Confidering it is requifite and
conuenient his Souldiers, rather then to imploy themfelues in fuch quarrels, fhould indeauour and aduenture
their bodies to ouerthrow and kill the enemie, thereby to
procure his owne proper praife and peculiar profite. Alwaies prouided, that the occafion of the warres be con-
cluded and publifhed to be lawfull and honeft, which
eafily in this refpect doth remoue all difficulties, whilft a
man doth place himfelfe in the feruice of a Prince that is
religious, prudent, and iuft, and that haue expreffe and
lawfull power to leuie armes, and not with thofe which
are of fmall authoritie, or tiranous Vfurpers of other
mens ftates, and wicked bloud fuckers.

Therefore when the Lieutenant cannot by his owne
dealings fupply thefe wants, or pacifie and accord them,
in fuch caufes he may remit the care thereof vnto his Superiour and Captaine. And thus let him haue fpeciall
care that by his meanes no quarrels do grow, neither that
he fuffer any faction or difcention, to take deepe roote,
for feare of banding and mutinies.

O   He

He ought to haue fpeciall refpect that the Corporals and Sergeants be able duly to execute their office with due diligence for the better performance of feruice, and perfonally aide them in fetting the watch.

Likewife, to the intent that the *Sergeant* perfift not ignorantly, or faile in any one point of his office : it be-houes the Lieutenant in many particular points to aide him, both in refpect of his owne credite, and for the generall benefit of the whole band: as in vfing diuers di-rections, difciplines, inuentions, putting the band in or-der, ranke, fquare, in accompanying them to the watch, and in executing fuch like enterprifes which commonly are to be performed.

. So ought he likewife to delight himfelfe extraordinari-ly (befides the other neceffary parts of his office) in taking view of the Corps de gard, and the Sentinels of his proper company, to the intent they may remaine con-tinually vigilant and ready, and each mans duty ducly executed, the martiall lawes read and examined, and a folemne filence generally maintained.

He muft obferue great affabilitie and fraternitie with the *Alfierus,* and friendly confult with him (fpecially if the Lieutenant doth not manage both the one and the o-ther office, as the *Spaniards* and other nations doe vfe, and might very well be vfed of vs, if the Generall or Co-ronell thinke good, both for auoiding of emulation and charge of pay) but if they be two particular Officers, and beare diftinct fway in the band, then let the Lieutenant be very carefull (as he that is the chiefe) to auoide all ftomaking and ftrife that might arife betwixt him and the *Alfierus,* for thereby oftentimes great fcandales haue falne out, and the diuifion of the company, a thing aboue

all

all other to be carefully forefeene and fhunned. Hee
ought to vfe a gratious gefture, and a curteous entertain-
ment to all his fouldiers, countenance euery one ioyful-
ly, and folicite their caufes carefully towards the Captaine and the other Officers, as the Treafurers, Pay-
mafters, Commiffaries and fuch like, yet euer by the
Captaines confent, yea and to the Captaine himfelfe, by
whofe friendly fauour inferiour Officers may be relieued
for their pay or other wants. Befides he ought to giue order and direction to all the company, diuiding and diftributing the fquadres indifferently and difcretly, to the
intent the Corporals and other Officers may be obeyed,
and that each enterprife may be performed without reply or contradiction.

It is neceffarie that he put in euery Squadre an equall
number of euery fort of armes, and that each weapon be
forted in a readineffe, to the intent that in what place and
time foeuer occafion doth require, euery one of them
may to his great aduantage, proceed and front the inuading enemie with a forceable ftrength.

Likewife it is good fometimes not to fuffer a fquadre
or rather a whole Corps de gard to confift of fouldiers
all of one Countrey and nation, but ought rather to bee
artificially mixed, and to feparate them thereby to auoid
quarrell and generalitie of factions, which by reafon of
their being together may the rather arife amongft con-
forts of one natiue Countrie, and that more commodioufly then if they were feparated.

The Captaine being abfent, the Lieutenant poffeffeth
the principall and chiefe place, and ought to be obeyed
as Captaine Neuertheleffe in his prefence, it is requifite
he vfe a certaine brotherly friendfhip and familiaritie to-

wards

wards all, yet that notwithstanding, he must proceede in all things with such modestie and grauity, as he may retaine such authoritie and reputation, as the office he doth hold, doth most worthily inuest him withall.

There ought to be in him a reasonable good knowledge and facilitie in expressing his conceit and meaning sensibly, that the souldiers may vnderstand what they haue to doe, to the intent he may the more easily imprint in the hearts and mindes of his Souldiers all such things as hee determines, and that be necessarie for the better seruice of his Prince, and the benefit of his Countrey and company, whereunto hee ought to apply himselfe with all possible diligence, since that of the Prince he is liberally paid, hath his being of his Countrey, and is diligently obeyed of his Band, where he swaies his present office and charge, which is truely of great credit and no lesse commoditie.

Let him prouide himselfe of a horse to beare him, to the intent he may be lusty and fresh in all enterprises, and that he may continually take the view and diligently suruey the order which they are to keepe in marching, or in making Alta, and at all other times besides in what enterprise soeuer.

He must take order that his baggage or carriage, which ought to be as little as may be (which rule the common Souldiers ought likewise obserue) be borne and conuaide amongst the common cariage which the Captaine hath ordained and prouided for the vse of the whole band.

He must take diligent care to the redeeming of prest or lent money, which the Captaine shall make according to occasion or neede amongst the company, and to distribute the same conueniently amongst the Souldiers, and
thereof

thereof to render and yeeld good account to the Captaine, by doing whereof he fhall pleafure the Souldiers
much, in which time of pay, he hath very good oportu-
nitie to put the Souldiers in minde, and to teach them to
proceed in well doing, and to defift from euill.

It appertaines generally to euery Lieutenant of a band
to be of great experience and ripeneffe of feruice, whofe
authoritie in the abfence of the Captaine (as partly I
touched before) extendeth to examine,trie,reforme, cor-
rect, and amend any offence committed within the band,
and alfo day and night to bring the company with the
Enfigne to the place of affembly, there in order traine
and exercife the fame, as to the neceffity of feruice doth
appertaine,and being commanded by the higher powers
to march towards the enemie, muft encounter and fight
with them, as if the Captaine were in prefence,who vpon
impediment, muft fometimes be abfent.

Finally, it appertaines to the Lieutenant to watch,
ward, approach, conduct, aduance againft the enemies,
and to encounter, animate, comfort, and alfo to encourage the company by word and deed as need ferueth : to
retire continually maintaining skirmifh, vntill he haue re-
couered fome place of fafegard.

Chap. IV.

*The office and dutie that appertaines to Lanze-fpezzate, vo-
luntarie Lieutenants, the Gentlemen of a Band, or Caualliers of S. Georges fquadrons.*

THe fundry degrees whereunto valiant Souldiers
with afpiring mindes feeke to afcend, for that they

O 3 be

be many,and for that thofe which haue attained and ferued in thofe roomes and other great offices, by diuers finifter meanes and accidents, be now and then diffeuered
and made fruftrate from their charge, as experience hath
made many times apparant, who yet neuertheleffe being
naturally defirous to continue in feruice, and perchance
through forraine neceffitie are driuen to remaine in pay,
in attending further preferment : Therefore this place
was firft inuented for fuch perfons, as a fpeciall feat
wherein the flower of warlike foldiers do fit,like a greene
Lawrell garland that doth environ the martiall head of a
mighty Armie, whofe order for warlike force or fame,
giues not place to the Græcian Phalanges, the chiefeft of
the Romane Legions, or to the knightly conftitution or
couragious enterprifes of thofe of *Arthurs* round table.
For there neither hath bin, nor can be found any place
of honor or reputation, as to be a Gentleman of a Band,
whether we ferue for pleafure or for profit, or haue attained thereunto by merit : or whether we haue bin Corporall, Sargeant, Alfierus, or Lieutenant, wherein Captaines
fometimes do plant themfelues, fpecially in the Colonels
Squadre, and temporife the time, vntill preferment doe
fall : for thereby their former reputation is nothing dif-
graced, nor their charge had, in or of any other company,
nothing derogated : Confidering that thofe in thefe
Squadrons, either are or ought to be foldiers of fuch policie and perfit experience, that they be capable of any
office vnder the degree of a Colonell, and may fupply
any of thofe forefaid offices, or performe any other enterprife of great importance commanded by the Captaine, Colonell, or Generall.

And for that many youths of noble parentage, and
Gentlemen

Gentlemen of ancient houses doe likewise follow the warres, I would that vpon due tryall of their merit, they should enter into these Squadrons, which the Prince or Generall is to confirme, and make a distinct order of valiant aduentrous soldiers, and call them Caualliers of *S. Georges* Squadrons, or some such other title; at whose entrance thereinto, they shall take a solemne oath appertayning to their order, and their Corporall shall invest them with some Bandroll, Medall or Scarfe, whereupon is pourtrayed *S. George* his armes, which they must be bound to weare openly at all times, and in all places, enterprises, skirmishes, battailes, and assaults. I do not put this title for a generall rule, but only as an example for instance, the title may be as authoritie shall thinke fit.

It is requisite that a singular good soldier, being the Gentleman of a band, and Cauallier of *S. George* his squadron, if he meane to gaine the grace and fauour of his Captaine and Colonell, that not onely he be sufficiently valiant and wise, as of necessitie is required at his hands: but it is also conuenient for him to be reasonable well horsed, and to haue in store all sorts of armes, as a Halberd, Harquebuse for the match or fire-locke, Armour and Target of proofe, his Lance and case of Pistolets, his Pike, his Pertisan or Epien to go the Round withall, that he may both day and night varie and change his armes at the offer of all enterprises, and as change of seruice doth call him forth.

He must alwaies of necessitie haue more than one seruant, and ought to apparell him in gallant order: these are to be neere his elbow to follow him with his armes. He ought alwaies to lodge himselfe as neere as is possible, to the lodging of his Colonell or Captaine, to the intent
that

that either armed, or without armes, he may alwayes, according as the cause doth require, be about his person, either on horseback or on foot; for that the principall guard of this singular personage, that is to say, the Colonell or Captaine, doth consist in the diligence and custody of the Caualliers of *S. George* his squadrons: for so I will be bold to call them, though the title be to be varied. These things notwithstanding, day and night when it fals to his lot, or that he shall be commanded by his Corporall to watch, he must dispose himselfe to be able to make particular guard, and that after a most exquisite order: wherein he must haue speciall care (without making refusall at any time) to performe that which shall be appointed him by his Corporall, or by any other that shall command in the name of his Colonell or Captaine. His office in time of watch, for the most part, consists in going the Round, searching the watch, keeping good order in the Corps of Guard, in being a Coadiutor to the officer that guides the company, or rules the watch, and is for the most part exempted from standing Sentinell, and such like duties of a common soldier, vnlesse great necessitie or speciall seruice constraine. It appertaines to him to haue good experience in going the Round, that in performing the same, he may discreetly gouerne in the ouersight of the watch, called the *Sopraguardia*: for in this point doth very much consist the prouident good order and forme that is to be obserued, in auoyding the stratagems, surprises, sallies, and deceits of the enemie. Approching neere to the Sentinell, he must giue eye and diligent regard in what order and sort he doth finde him vigilant, how ready he is in demanding and taking the word, and after comming neerer him, he must examine
all

all that hath paffed or fallen out whileft he hath bin in
Sentinell, and the order he doth obferue, and what hath
bin appointed him to doe : the which if it be good he
muft confirme, and when he doth finde it to be otherwife, he muft reherfe and refer the fame to the Corporall of the Sentinell, that he may vfe diligent redreffe.

Arriuing in any Corps de guard, he muft aboue all
things aduertife them, that they alwaies keepe fire light
for the neceffarie commoditie of the Harquebufiers, and
for light in the night, taking order with the foldiers that
they and their armes may remaine in a forcible readines :
through which his good inftruction, there may grow to
be no want, and fo confequently he muft in like cafes
proceed with like prouident diligence.

After this he muft with great confideration and modeftie, examine euery particular thing, carrying a minde
with himfelfe to continue and increafe the fame from
better to better, and both in himfelfe and to them vfe neceffarie aduertifements, and in fuch fort fhall he paffe
through all the Corps de guards, and Sentinels.

If it chance him to incounter another *Sopraguardia* or
Round, to fhun the occafion of dangerous difference,
which fometimes is accuftomed to follow : or for policie, in fearing to giue the watch-word to him that purpofely comes to rob the fame, that comming from the
enemy fecretly, counterfeits the Sentinell, or by fome
other practife, as it fometimes hath caufed damage to
the grieuous loffe and totall preiudice of the Armie : to
preuent fuch inconuenience, let that *Sopraguardia* which
fhall be neereft to the next adioyning Sentinell, turne
backe, giuing the word after a due accuftomed fort vnto
the faid Sentinell, to the intent the forefaid *Sopraguardia*

P   may

may do the like, and when they are of accord, euery one may follow his owne path; but if otherwife they doe difagree, the deceit remaines difcouered, not only in that counterfeit Round, but alfo in the fained Sentinell, whom the *Sopraguardia* muft examine, and demand at his hand fome fpeciall counterfigne or double word, that thereby he may know him for an affured friend, or finde him an enemy or negligent perfon, the which of all men is very well knowne to merit fharpe and extreame chaftifement, which at no time, fo neere as is poffible, is to be omitted.

This former rule is to be obferued of thofe foldiers that be of one felfe nation: but when the Rounds or Sopraguards be many and of fundry Nations, and the Corps of guards likewife; then the Sopraguard comming into a quarter that is ftranger vnto him, is bound to giue the word to the Sopraguard of that nation, and of that quarter; fo that by fuch meanes as well the fufpition of deceit, as the occafion of difcord fhall be auoyded.

And if in cafe the faid ordinarie Round or Sopraguard, do incounter in their owne quarter, with the extraordinary, thofe that be ordinary fhall indeuour themfelues to take the word of thofe that be extraordinarie: for fo it is conuenient, and moft conformable to that order before-faid, wherein I haue fet downe what is neceffarie for a Sopraguard or Round to do in a ftrange quarter. And for that it is requifite, as I haue already touched, that the Caualliers be alwaies about the perfon of his chiefe Captaine, without either being bound to Standerd, Guidon, or other Enfigne whatfoeuer, he muft indeuour himfelfe, when any enterprife or warlike affaires is committed to his charge, to be apt and ready to vfe

practifed

practifed experience in directing and guiding a skirmifh, in taking the view of a battery, in difcouering of the enemy, in marching or making Alta, in Paffa parde in the valiant repulfe of a fodaine inuading enemie by *Bawl en bouche*, in taking view of the fituation of a place, in guiding a Roade, or troupe of horfemen, in giuing alarme to the enemie, in plucking aduertifements from the enemy, in placing Imbafcades, in giuing Canvafadoes, and to know very well how to execute with found iudgement thefe and fuch like important affaires, the which for the moft part appertaine to the Caualliers of this Squadron to performe. As likewife it hath bin the cuftome to giue them the charge for to plant *Gabiones* for the defence of the Artillery, to batter and endomage the walles, the trenches, the lodgings, and the enemies Squadrons.

Let him remember when he hath bin at any exploit, to bring backe againe into his quarter, thofe foldiers he hath led forth to any enterprife, vnited and in ranke, marching togither behind him, and neuer fuffer them to returne difbanded one by one out of order, which is an occafion of great confufion, and brings but fmall reputation to the Captaine and conductor of them.

Moreouer, it is very neceffarie he know how to make a roade and deftroy the enemies country; the which likewife doth oftentimes appertaine to him to performe: in which exploit he muft beware aboue all things, that no foldier in thofe enterprifes difperfe or difband themfelues, but with an affured good order, for the moft part conformable to my following difcourfe, wherein I fet downe directions, how to conduct foldiers to the skirmifh: and particularly where I declare that he ought to keepe and maintaine for his people the ftrongeft place

of

of fituation, wherein he muft skirmifh ; for that commonly foldiers being in diforder, wearied and laden with fpoile, may be eafily put to flight, broken and oppreffed of the enemies, vnleffe they be feconded or fhaded by fome forceable fuccour.

I fuppofe it likewife moft neceffarie, that he indeuour himfelfe to be apt and fufficient at all times, and in all places to follicite and negotiate for his Prince or Chieftaine, any caufe of what weight or moment foeuer, confidering that moft men are not fit to attempt the performance of fuch doubtfuli and difficile caufes : for although many make great eftimation of themfelues, and prefume much by their daily reading and Theoricke of thofe weighty affaires, yet do they want and come far fhort of that bold and ready practife, which plainely appeares, that the worthy profeffors of Armes poffeffe ; and fpecially in the prefence of great Princes, whofe maieftie and reuerence for the moft part, doth make cold and bring out of countenance the hotteft & moft refolute determination : as *Demofthenes* before *Philip* of *Macedone* made apparent, when he was not able to pronounce three words of a long premeditated Oration, in behalfe of the *Athenians*.

This worthy Gentleman of a band, this Cauallier of *S. Georges* fquadre, and likewife all other profeffors of warlike armes, ought to carry in minde, that of him and his equals the exercife of Armes is to be applied, and diligently to practife the fame, to the intent he be not for want of knowledge defpifed of others ; and not ignorantly to defpife them that deferue due commendations, but rather to carry and vfe the countenance of authoritie to thofe perfons that merit not to beare fway and gouernment, than towards forward foldiers : Yet for all
that

that towards the relt in fome other refpeets, he ought to
gratifie them and helpe them to his power, and fo courteoufly winne the goodwils and freindly fauour of all
fouldiers his equals,to inftruct and courteoufly to admonifh euery Souldier priuately and apart,what appertaines
to his dutie. This Caualliere muft be able alfo to traine
fouldiers, to make them march in orderly proportions, to
caft them in ringes, effes, fnailes, hearfes, fquadres, to receiue and giue charge, to faine skirmifhes, onfets, re-
traites, and how to order any number of fouldiers, from
a hundreth to fiue hundreth, for fo many may be in a
Band, and vnder one Enfigne, as the *Swizers* and *Germaines* yet vfe at this day, and as in former ages our
Countrimen haue vfed,which in fome refpeets may paffe
without reprehenfion. If a Captaine be difpofed to haue
fo many vnder his Enfigne, when he is not able to bring
the number vnto a whole Collonifhip, together with the
knowledge of the order how to traine,he muft indeauour
himfelfe to be perfit in drawing platformes, in the Ma-
thematikes, in the martiall Lawes,in befieging of townes,
batteries, mines, and each thing elfe belonging to martiall difcipline.

Let this worthy Cauallier of *Saint Georges* fquadre
haue then before his eyes fuch like precepts, and manage
of martiall affaires, that he may encreafe his owne credit,
winne his countrey fame, fauour of his Prince, and honour of his houfe and friends, rather then for the regard
of riches, ftately houfes, liuings, and fuch like, but rather
preferre prudent policie, courage, valour and approued
experience before fuch bafe benefits, whereby hee may
attaine to the Lawrell crowne, wherewith diuers mighty
Conquerors haue their heads adorned : that hee may be

an

an example to the reproach of such as lewdly spend their daies in idlenesse, prodigalitie, lust and obloquie.

Chap. V.

The office of a Captaine which hath the guiding of a Band of men.

THat person which hath the charge to gouerne other men, specially in matters of weight and of great importance, the liues of men being committed to his hands, vnder whose conduct if any quaile through rashnesse or want of knowledge, he is bound to render account before God: and therefore he ought to be of notable capacitie, experience, and exemplar in all his actions and enterprises, since it is a generall note that the eyes of all those that be subiects, be turned towards their principall head and chiefe, in whom as it were in a glasse, they retaine an assured hope to behold most ready rules and perfit examples, whereby they may guide and gouerne themselues.

In this particular charge of a Captaine, the qualitie of his Officers, make almost a manifest shew of his valour and experience: Therefore like an old and expert Souldier, as one that hath past through all those degrees and offices set downe in my two former bookes, he must vse a circumspect care in leuying and making choise of his company, that is, to make election of a politike and practised Lieutenant, of a couragious Alfierus, of a carefull Sergeant, of gallant and valiant Caualliers of his squadre, of valiant Corporals, of a diligent Chancellour, Secretarie,

rie, or Clarke of the Band, of a faithfull Furrier or Harbinger, being of good iudgement and confideration, and of a *Surgion* prouided of all things neceffarie to minifter according to his arte. But aboue all things let him prouide to retaine in his Band a Preacher, or fuch a perfon which may take care to minifter the Communion to the Souldiers, and fpecially to roote obedience in their hearts : who likewife euery day may celebrate diuine feruice, which euen from the beginning hath beene vfed of the Church. And finally muft haue for euery hundreth a practifed Drummer of good vnderftanding.

When he hath gathered and vnited his companie, the whole Band being prefent, his Minifter muft deuoutly read certaine praiers, and afterward the Enfigne fhall be publikely placed in the hands, and recommended to the cuftodie of the Alfierus, and as in my former difcourfe of this point, command him to haue as much care thereof, as of his proper life, honour and credite, which hee ought couragioufly to aduance and difplay, to prefer his party in a rightfull quarrell , according to my fpeech where I fet downe his duty. This done he muft priuately make election amongft his chiefeft Souldiers of fo many Caualliers or Lancia Spezzata, that is to fay, Gentlemen of his Band, as may amount to the number of two out of euery fquadre. Some nations vfe 50. to a fquadre, as the Suitzers and Germaines, fome others leffe, according to their difcretion : but in my opinion 25. is a more conuenient number, both for that the Corporall may the more often and with greater diligent care inftruct and fee to his charge, then if they were 50. Befides 25. fouldiers diuided into 5. rankes makes a iuft fquare, fo that by the fame account 300. may containe 12. fquadres,

dres, and euery one haue a Corporall of the same number : whereof 10. Corporalls haue the leading of mixt
weapons, the 11. charge ouer the Halberdiers, and the
12. to consist of Gentlemen, old and expert Souldiers,
amongst whom the targets of proofe ought to be in number. The Captaine at the same time, when he appoints
his Ensigne, must likewise solemnly constitute and confirme a Corporall ouer the Caualliers of his squadre,
which he may entitle of Saint *George*, and enroll their
names by this title, the Corporall and Caualliers of
of *S. George* his squadre. He may inuest and bestow vpon the Corporall a scarfe of red and white sarsnet, and a
Medall or iewell of gold or siluer double gilt, wherein
the portrature of *S. George* is liuely wrought, to hang a-
bout his necke, at his scarfe or otherwise : and moreouer
to him and all the rest of the squadre he may giue a little
Phane or Penon of silke vpon a wire, whereof the Crosse
must be of red, and the rest of the square white, the other
part of the sarsenet of the Captaines coulors, or with
what words, or deuise therein shall please him best : They
must weare this behind, either vpon their burganets, or
vpon their hats if they will in a plume of red and white
feathers, specially in all enterprises and warlike attempts:
Besides this vpon their cassockes or mandillions towards
their right brest a red crosse of veluet, satten or scarlet,
imbrothered or comely stitched, that they may appeare
manifestly and be knowne from the rest of the Souldiers,
like worthy Guides and Leaders, whose courage and valour may incite others to ascend to their dignitie and
degree.

They must solemnly promise, vow and sweare to their
possibilitie, not onely to be the first to force the breach of

a

a battered towne, trench, or fortreſſe, to giue the firſt couragious onſet vpon the maine battaile, or the enemies ſquadrons, to peirce a paſſage, and gallantly guide the Souldiers to the skirmiſh, to ſuddaine ſallies, ſurpriſes, eſcalados, canuaſados, and ſuch like, but alſo to obſerue, maintaine, and inſtruct the ignorant in all militarie directions, obſeruations, and martiall lawes of the field.

In reſpect hereof thoſe that be Caualliers and Gentlemen of this ſquadre, muſt be intertained with a ſtipend and greater pay then the common Souldier, and with other notable ſignes of manifeſt difference, by reaſon they either are or ought to be the beſt and moſt practiſed Souldiers in his whole band: for this word Lancia ſpezzata amongſt the *Italians*, is of no other ſignification, then a tried experience in the warres. To which Caualliers he may freely and faithfully with great confidence and truſt, commit the charge of any office in his companie that is vacant, or the performance of any other enterpriſe or accident, and may if he will tearme them extraordinary Lieutenants, which he muſt alwaies haue about him vpon any ſodaine to execute his commandement, and ſupply other offices when time ſhall ſerue.

A Captaine ought to haue ſpeciall and particular knowledge of all thoſe things that appertaine to the office of a Lieutenant, and the office of an Alfierus, which if he thinke good he may linke both in one, for amongſt diuers nations now a daies, one man commonly ſupplies both their offices.

The office and dutie of the Sergeants of the Caualliers of S. *Georges* ſquadre, whom he muſt eſteeme as extraordinarie Lieutenants of the Corporals, Clarke of the Band, Harbinger, Drummes and Fifes: and finally, the

Q   dutie

dutie of euery particular and common Souldier, that he may prefently redreffe any thing amiffe, and vpon any new accident to inftruct them either in marching, encamping, or fighting, fo that he may be able to command them, according as time, place, and reafon doth require, without contradiction or appointing that to be done of one Officer, which ought to be done of an other : or that he doth command them to doe things not conuenient, and much leffe that which is not lawfull or not honourable. Which order of proceeding doth very much difpleafe and bring men of warre in miflike of fuch vndirect dealings. Since the principall point and practife whereunto their exercife in armes doth tend, is to attaine reputation, honour, and credite, he muft continually court his Collonell and Cheiftaine, forcing himfelfe to be one of the firft that doth falute him in the morning, and of the laft to depart from him in the euening, that thereby hee may be fufficiently inftructed and informed in euery particular act and practife, which is to be put in execution, touching the performance of any enterprife or warlike act, fince that in thofe cafes a wary man may beft take hold of occafion, whereof he ought to make triall in time of warre, the which he is likewife to accomplifh, afwell for the feruice of his cheife and Prince, as alfo for his owne fatisfaction, and the honour, benefit, and reputation of his Souldiers.

Let him in fome fort prouide with as much aduantage and commodity as he can, that his fouldiers baggage be alwaies conducted from place to place, alwaies prohibiting fuperfluitie, and in long voiages their corflets and armes of heauie burthen : prouided that he march not in fufpected places, and in the enemies countrie, but not otherwife. Let

Let him take order that his Souldiers be light in apparell, fo that it be warme, and haue as little baggage and otherwife loaden as may be, to the intent they may vfe all their diligence about their weapons, and not to hale backe for feare of loofing the fame, but rather haue refpect to the warie keeping of their armes, and that they may rather be more bent and determined to fight, in hope of gaine and honour, then fufpected thorough the doubt of loofing that which they already poffeffe.

He muft not be couetous, neither retaine one penie of pay from his Souldiers, but rather diftribute amongft them, all the aduantages, dead paies, and capifoldi: to the intent they may be well paied and rewarded which merite the fame, fo fhall he gaine honour and make them affured in perillous feruice.

Let him reftraine fouldiers from hauing horfes, thereby to auoide confufion, for that commonly euery one muft march about the Enfigne, to the intent the rankes be not broken and difturbed by horfes: And that Souldiers be not occupied in going abroad for forrage for their horfes, as of neceffitie they muft, which is proper to Horfemen and not to footmen, but onely thofe which are to be permitted with the Lieutenant, the Alfierus, and fome of the Caualliers of *Saint Georges* fquadre, that are Gentlemen of greateft experience, for that they may ferue in fteed and place of light horfemen, to view, difcouer, conduct and carie a meffage or commandement with great fpeed, when and where need doth require.

It is neceffary for him to haue fome knowledge and fight in making bulwarkes, trenches, platformes, skonces, fortreffes, and fuch like, and to know the nature and qualitie of them, afwell that with aduantage he may bee

able

able to know how to affault, as alfo to make them with facilitie, in times and places moft neceffarie : which vnderftanding and Art, is particularly conuenient for him, confidering the defence of men of warre in the field, for the moft part confifts afwell in trenches, bulwarkes, and perfect platformes, as in good and well gouerned fquadre and in maine battaile.

He muft haue with him a paire of lanthornes for the campe, fome creffets, linkes, or torches that blow not out with the winde, and fuch like to vfe in the night, and in ftormes and tempefts for feruice of the company, as in roundes, alarmes &c. And for his proper commoditie and ornament a pauillion or tent of fufficient capacitie, veffels to accommodate his victuals, and furniment for the fire and kitchin, of fmall weight and difturbance in cariage, and certaine houfhold ftuffe neceffarie for himfelfe and his traine, to the intent he may fo neere as is pofsible commodioufly make fupplie to the continuation of things requifite for victuals. He ought alwaies to lodge with his Band, and remaine with the fame both in good and euill, and continually fhew himfelfe louing and courteous, and take fuch part as the Souldiers doe : for contrariwife, taking his eafe, and fuffering them to be lodged or fedde miferably, breedeth him hatred or contempt.

Neither ought hee to fhunne toile and trauaile, but carefully take delight and liking to be alwaies the firft, that with prouident prudence doth lay his hand to any worke, or performe any enterprife which is conuenient to be done : for that for the moft part the rude ftubborne multitude of Souldiers is not conftrained and forced fo much, to doe his dutie by compulfion, as they be voluntarie moued thereunto through fhame, and a reuerent
refpect

refpect they haue to the example of their Superiour. Neither let the practife of the fame be painefull vnto him, for that to liue at eafe and to be curious of his owne commodious being, and fuffer his Souldiers taft the toiles of trauaile, is rather the order of a delicate Prince, then of a carefull and couragious Captaine.

Let him not faile euery night that he is of the watch, to fend his Sergeant to take the word fecretly of the Sergeant maior, (wherewith the watch of that night ought to be gouerned) or of fome other that fhall be appointed to giue it, which hee muft vfe wifely and warily, fince that negligence in like cafes may be the ruine of him and his company, and confequently of a whole armie. Hee muft haue tried experience, and full practife in all the points noted of me in my firft booke, and be perfit in the conduct of martiall affaires, that with great facilitie hee may be able to know, and with great aduife to deale in all the particulars belonging to all the degrees of fouldiers vnder his eftate, and of leffe eftimation then a Captaine.

It behoues him to carie a valiant and couragious heart, that vpon all fuddaines he may be able to execute all enterprifes, and that hauing ouer-viewed, ordered and difpofed thofe things that be neceffary, he may be able to execute the fame with fuch prompt and ready dexteritie, as appertaines to the terrible and bloudy accidents of armes. And although there be very few who haue fuch happy fucceffe, as they may be accounted fortunate and politike both together: Neuertheleffe it is requifite he be prudent, and difcipher and looke before hand into fuch things as are like to fall out, that he may with difcreete modefty vfe either good or euill fortune, whether foeuer

Q 3 fhall

shall arise: for the life of man is to be compared to the play at Tables, in the which the player may desire and deuise which is the best cast, but yet which way soeuer the dice turne, either good or euill, he ought with as great discretion and arte as he can, accommodate himselfe and serue his turne withall. He should possesse and be indued with a noble minde, that he may alwaies haue the same inclined to discreet liberalitie, and not to nigardly couetousnes, by which vice we see many incurre and fall into most opprobrious chances, into treasons and pernicious rebellions, which are men worthy of most shamefull corrections.

I iudge it likewise very necessarie for him to be eloquent, since that qualitie hath great efficacie in perswading of mens mindes, which oftentimes haue much need to be wakened and pricked forward with a spurre, specially in those terrible accidents that fall out in the exercise of armes, which in painfull perilous actions would otherwise languish, faint, and become fearefull. Therefore let the loue towards God, the care of their Country, their present perill, the example of magnanimitie in their forefathers, the quarrell, cause, and benefits to soule & body, be meanes to make them valiantly accomplish their acts. He ought neuer to make conference, concerning that which he is to put in execution, neither of any one thoght imagination, or inuention appertaining to the state of those warlike attempts and affaires, but with those persons, of whom he may assuredly reserue faithfull and friendly counsell; for that the importance of such and so great dealings, ought euer to be had in suspition of discouerie. Therefore a wise and carefull man will euer haue a warie and iealous eye ouer such weighty affaires.

Now

Now the order for him to punifh his foldiers in cafes wherein they are not guilty of death, I thinke the moft important punifhment which appertaines to the Captaine to giue them, is openly amidft the whole company and band, fhamefully to difarme them, to take away their money and chiefeft garments, and fo to banifh them and fend them packing: for to put them to death, or furioufly to beat them, belongs to the office of the Mafter of the Campe and Marfhall of the field, and not to the Captaine; for if he fhould beat his foldiers, he fhould make himfelfe hated and embafe himfelfe, and bring his foldiers either to become mutinous or abiects. Note, that it is not fufficient onely for a Captaine to haue ordained his Company difcreetly, and therein to haue great numbers of good men, which is to fay, in warlike affaires valiant men: but aboue all things it is very neceffarie when he fhall come to blowes and fight, he fhould aduenture and performe the fame to his manifeft aduantage, or elfe conftrained thereunto by pure neceffitie, although he ought to flie the laft fo much as he is able, obferuing this for a generall rule, not to fight either by chance, either for pleafure, or for ambition, as many times we fee done by rafh and ambitious Chiefes and Captaines.

Moreouer, he muft worke in fuch fort, that his foldiers haue very good occafion and apt means to win the victory, and that they be frefh and luftie, to the intent that in fighting they may ouercome: for without thefe and like aduertifements by tempting fortune, men for the moft part both loofe, and are ouerthrowne.

It is very conuenient he procure the hauing of an ample and autentike Patent of his Colonell, with as large words of fauour as may be, wherein muft be declared at
the

the inftance and appointment of what Prince the expedition is made, and fo with modeftie and prudence he fhall
vfe the authoritie that is giuen him, but neuerthelesse
there, as it behoues him fo to doe.

It is not requifite that in all places he fuffer his Enfigne
to be difplayed; the manner and doing whereof fhewes
force and authoritie, the which many times is not to be
vfed, neither in each place : when a man is inferior to o-
thers, he ought to vfe great dexteritie and modeftie, which
euer fals out both to be commodious and commendable.

And moreouer according to the order of *Paffa parole*,
of aduertifements from mouth to mouth, he ought euer
to obferue a filent and affured plaine information to his
whole band, whereby they may vpon the fodaine alter
aray, make *alta* , march flow or faft, clofe or in wide
ranks, or prepare their peece, match and bullet for a fuddaine Alarme, inuafion, skirmifh, or defence.

A Captaine that muft leuie a band is to make his election and choife of his officers and foldiers, not only approued and fufficiently experienced , but alfo vfe fuch
fpeedy march in his expedition and iourney, that he may
ioyne his company to the reft of the Armie, at or before
the appointed day and place.

When he may march by land with his company, let
him neuer defire to goe by fea, hoping to fpare coft and
fhorten time; for by becomming fubiect to the indifcre-
tion of the winde, either through long abode, or fome
accident by fhipwrack or tempefts, there hath rifen many
times great difturbance and ruine without remedie, fince
by this defect many good occafions, and of great importance haue bin loft and made fruftrate.

He ought neuer to take iourney in hand without a
guide,

guide, the which he muſt procure to be giuen him by the Chiefe that doth command him, to the intent he may alwaies remaine excuſed and faultleſſe from thoſe errors, that by ſuch defects may or do commonly ariſe ; which diligence is not onely particularly to be vſed, when any iourney of ſmall length is to be guided, but if any long iourney is to be made (not being able to do better) he muſt circumſpectly haue him alwaies by his ſide, neither ought to haue him ſlip away from him or abſent, ſince that euery ſmall error or going out of the way in a iourney and marching, doth diſpleaſe ſoldiers and warlike perſons, and yeelds leſſe reputation to the Captaine, who ought alwaies to march with them , and to prouide and procure through his authoritie all things neceſſarie, with the greateſt fauour and aduantage poſſible.

He ought alwaies to keepe his ſoldiers exerciſed, by often view and muſter of them, marching ſometimes along in rankes by 3. 5. 7. and 9. &c. in a ranke : ſometime in trayning them in Rings, Eſſes, Dees, Battailes, Squadrons, turning one rank throughan other, in leading them to skirmiſh, & in ſuch ſort practiſe them daily. And alſo he muſt cauſe his ſoldiers to ſhoot vollees of ſhot, ſometimes all at once, ſometimes by rankes, and ſometimes mixed : the which vollees vpon the ſigne or ſound of drum, or word of mouth by the Captaine muſt be accompliſhed with celeritie, and cloſely togither and cunningly, and not out of diſorder or by peeces , a great while one after another, but vpon their diſcharge, ioyntly togither ; without rumor, noiſe or tumult they muſt all charge againe, and vpon a ſigne giuen by the Captaine, giue a freſh vollee &c.

R   He

He muft likewife delight to fee them well armed with all forts of armes, euery one according to the weapon he beares: and fometimes likewife exercife them in running, leaping, wraftling, throwing the barre, and ordinarily caufe them to be wakened in the morning betimes, charging the drums to ftrike the Diana throughout the whole quarter.

A Captaine may at all times accompanie his band with the found of drum and fife, which muft giue order to their continuall march, and directs all their other enterprifes, vnleffe to accompany prifoners, to entrench, make plaine the way, to make and carry fagots, baskets, or gabions from the wood, and fuch like feruile and pefantly feruice, hardly digefted of honorable foldiers.

He to the intent he may be both loued and obeyed of his foldiers, muft apply himfelf to be prouident and politike in pacifying difcords, and all fuch difference as fhall arife amongft them, wherein if he finde any obftinate, fo foone as he hath performed his indeuour, and that thereby they will not agree and become friands, fo foone as their pay is ended, he ought to difcharge them. In times paft it hath bin vfed of notable Colonels to permit the combat, and caufe them to fight it out, thereby to extinguifh their obftination, to bridle their furie, and giue notable example to the reft: the which order although it hath bin tryed to auaile very much for their good gouernment, yet it is not to be vfed amongft Chriftians, Councells of Diuines hauing forbidden the fame; vnleffe to feare the parties he faigne that the fame fhall be performed of them to the vttermoft, and at the ioyning in fight to caufe them ftay, and take other order of punifhment, except they accord, and to difcharge them.

A

A Captaine ought to vſe all art and induſtry to invade, endomage,and ouerthrow the enemie, ſpecially infidels: and aboue all things to be franke of minde, and to feare nothing but diſhoneſt fame : likewiſe that he purchaſe authoritie amongſt his ſoldiers by meanes of vertue and valour ; let him procure by practiſe and effectuall experience to be accounted a wiſe and a worthy valiant Captaine, rather than to beare the name of a ſimple, weake, and vndiſcreet Colonell : for the name of a Captaine is a type and title of ſpeciall honor.

He muſt likewiſe in reſpect of a certaine inward deſire of emulation, not carie a baſe and abiect minde, but ſtill aſpiring with great ſubtiltie , by good inuention and induſtry, of a firme and faithfull diſpoſition, and neuer ſubiect to forgetfulnes, to the intent he may retaine in memory thoſe things that be well done,and all commendable enterpriſes, the which do marueilouſly and incredibly delight and feede mens mindes and diſpoſitions.

A Captaine muſt euer take care that his whole charge be ſtill furniſhed with men,armour,weapons and munitions, with all things needfull, and diſtributed at conuenient times.

He muſt ſuffer none through idleneſſe to neglect his armour, weapons and other furniture, whereby he ſhall grow vnready to ſeruice at neede, but giue his officers commandment circumſpectly to looke to the ſame.

Soldiers ſhould be prohibited from ouer-much liberty, neither to vſe whore-hunting, drunkenneſſe , common ſwearing, quarrelling,fighting,couſening,or ſuch like,but ſpeedy correction to be vſed.

Prouiſion of victuals,armour & munition being made, it muſt diſcreetly be vſed in due time by victuallers appointed,and to be diſtributed vnto the ſoldiers,and to ſee that the victuallers and other artificers, lending vnto ſol-diers vpon their credit at neede, vnt il their pay day, may be truely ſatisfied.

If any ſoldiers be taken priſoners, to be ranſomed home in due time, that his bands remaine not vnfur-niſhed.

Diuers points of ſeruice are committed to the Cap-taine, wherein great diſcretion and ſeruice is to be vſed, as in a Conuoy,Canuiſado,Ambuſh, Skirmiſh,Approch, Aſſault,retreit,ſurpriſe,paſſage of riuers,ſtreights, ſodaine fortifications, diſcoueries,&c. As in theſe and ſuch like occurrences, it is neceſſarie to vſe the aduiſe of expert ſoldiers, whoſe opinions are worthy to be obſerued, gra-tifying and rewarding them according to the value of their counſels. So likewiſe a Captaine muſt ſometimes proue, and circumſpectly try by fained pretences, affir-ming that he meanes to performe certaine exploits, and will march to ſome place, nothing intending the ſame, to the intent to diſcipher thoſe that be buſie-bodies, raſh and vnſecret in counſell, and ſuch as preſume without knowledge or experience; afterward reuealing the ſame, may try the truth and puniſh the offenders,as to his dutie and office is conuenient.

Chap. VI.
The Office of a Colonell.

A Valiant and worthy Colonell, after he hath a lawfull diſpatch of his Prince, and hath obtained his patent and preſt money, to conduct that number of ſoldiers his
charge

charge and expedition fhall containe, with all conuenient
diligence, and according as he is appointed, he muft make
election of as many Captaines as be needfull, diftributing
to euery one 300 for a band, which number is of moft
conuenient quantitie: for by reducing companies to a
leffe number, as in our time is vfed, fpecially amongft the
Spaniards and Italians, and followed by the French and
Englifh, they may rather carry the name of Lieutenants
and Centurions, than beare the title of Captaines. Befides
a band being made of a fmall number, the Treafurers
confume much more money amongft the great ftore of
officers, the which ought to be by all meanes poffible
auoyded of a politike Generall, and of a prudent Prince,
to auoide extraordinarie expence and confufion, which
doth eafily arife amongft the multitude of officers.

He muft be prouident to entertaine thofe that be old
Captaines, practifed, and bearing a good port, and that be
loued and defired of the foldiers, whom he ought to accompanie and prefer with the greateft authoritie he can
giue, with ample, fealed, and autentike Patents, thereby
more fpeedily and more eafily he may accomplifh his
affaires.

It is requifite he equally impart to euery one, the quantitie of that preft money he hath receiued, to the intent the
Captaine and the officers arife not to be burdened, taxed,
and confumed by ordinarie and extraordinarie meanes,
and other manifeft wayes about thofe affaires; and to
the intent the foldiers may tafte of beneuolence of their
Colonell: for by that meanes credit is fuftained, and his
traine augmented, a thing moft neceffarie to perfonages
that fupply fo great a place. For it is requifite that men
in the beginning be not difcouraged for want of neceffary

prouifion,

prouifion, yea rather to lend of his owne (confidering
he is to be paid againe) then his fouldiers fhould bee
brought to any extremity.

The diftribution of the preft-money ought to be preferred with great prudence , for afterwards at the banke,
the fame otherwife may be retained , and fubftraction
made of all the whole money , either in the firft pay or
thofe that follow, more or leffe as it feemes expedient,
principally for the vfe and commoditie of the fouldiers,
confidering (that according to the Prouerb) a man can
hardly at any time ferue two mafters , and therefore hee
muft ftand vpon this fpeciall point, to be more carefull
not to doe any thing preiudiciall to the honourable exercife of armes, then to pleafe the couetous and infatiable
humour of fome Captaines, whom in effect it pleafures
but little, in refpect their greedy defire is neuer fatisfied :
Neuertheleffe it falls out to bee a maruellous loffe and
hinderance to the enterprife, fpecially to men of valour
and fouldiers, without whofe aide a Collonell is but of
fmall force and value : And to conclude, money muft alwaies be procured, difperfed and fpent with great difcretion, order, and confideration , fince the fame is fo neceffarie to man, as it is called the finewes of warres.

It is a thing moft requifite that he carrie with him at
the leaft, one Minifter, a man of good life, who may exemplarly attend about the care of Ecclefiafticall matters,
wherein aboue all other things we ought thorowly to be
ftaid and inftructed.

He muft likewife haue in his regiment befides the ordinary Surgeons, an excellent and tried Phifition , well
prouided of all drugs and fpiceries, and of other things
neceffarie to be miniftred to thofe that be ficke.

His

His Lieutenant for his regiment muft be of a fingular qualitie and excellent experience, who not onely muft particularly gouerne his owne band and company, but alfo with great prudence and policie take care and charge ouer all the people which are in the bands vnder his Colonell, wherein the Lieutenant muft proceed according to my rules for the Lieutenant of a priuate band, and the notes in my fecond and third booke. His owne Alfierus as Generall and Superiour to the reft of the Enfigne-bearers vnder his Collonnelfhip, muft bee guided and gouerned by a fingular and fubftantiall fouldier, a Gentleman of an auncient houfe, courteous, wife and endowed with good conditions.

The fame order he ought likewife to obferue, in the election of his Caualliers of the fquadre, of his Sergeants, of his Corporalls, of his Drummers, and euery other Officer. It is a thing moft neceffary and conuenient, as in my fecond booke, and the office of a Captaine I haue touched, that a Collonell fhould retaine in his regiment, and fpecially in his owne band about him, a number of wife and worthy fouldiers, to be the Gentlemen of his company, Lance Spezzate, or ferue for extraordinarie Lieutenants, whom the Collonell muft not onely vfe and entreat well with an aduantage in their pay, but alfo feaft them, cherifh them, and fet them oftentimes by courfe at his owne table, and alwaies fhew them a courteous countenance, with which fhew of friendly courtefie, fouldiers be incredibly fedde, and contrariwife maruelloufly difpleafed with the hautie lookes of proud difdaine. For all thofe that make profeffion of this worthy Art, are of great curiofitie and courage, and therefore men of warre ought neuer (againft right) be villanoufly handled, either

ther in word, deed or countenance.

He muſt create a Sergeant Maior, that is a ſouldier of great experience, and that particularly is a profeſſour of that office, to the end he know preciſely what is to bee preferred in euery practiſe : ſuch a one as can yeeld thereof a perfect account and diſcourſe, and that conſequently can much better by deed then by word execute any enterpriſe. And for that in his office it is neceſſarie for him to vary and change purpoſe, with infinite aduertiſements and conſiderations, as the ſhortneſſe of time now and then requires, the diſcommoditie of the place and ſeat thereof doth inforce, the order of the enemies doth conſtraine, or according to his owne proper pollicie, or the prouident prudence of his Collonell : but for that this place doth not permit to ſpeake particularly of euery point, I will paſſe ouer the ſame, and onely referre all to the prouidence of his long and approued experience, which of neceſſitie is required vnto him, which I further referre to my following diſcourſe of the Sergeant Maior generall.

He ought to make a Marſhall of his lodgings, who muſt be his principall Furrier and Harbinger, that muſt attend with great diligence, to procure lodging for all, without pleaſing any one particular perſon for any priuate commoditie whatſoeuer, but muſt equally diſtribute, and depart the quarters and lodgings according as neede requires : neither is it to be borne withall, that hee doe make free any houſes or lodgings, neither go about any ſuch like gaine, a moſt diſhoneſt and vnlawfull robberie, which oftentimes doth cauſe great loſſe & diſcommoditie to men of warre, ſmall reputation to their Conductour, and great vexation and diſturbance to the poore
people,

people, who for the moft part are innocent. The Collo-
nels Harbinger hauing allotted out lodgings to euery
band he muft prefer the particular diftribution to the vnder Harbingers.

A generall Drummer ought likewife to be created and
appointed, who may take charge and care ouer all the reft
of the Drummers , whofe office and cuftome amongft
them is to conferue and keepe orders , to the intent they
may be obeyed , and that euery one performe his dutie
appertaining to his office, as to ftrike the batterie in marching in battaile, or diffeuered , to make generall bands
and cries, in the morning, in the euening at the cloling
of the night, and in founding the march, the call , the
charge, the battell, the retrait, with fuch other like obferuations and neceffarie things to be done.

He muft procure to haue part of euery munition for
his regiment,out of the principall and generall munition,
as corflets, pikes, halberds , hargabufes with their furniture, match, lead, pouder, of all fort of victuall, and each
thing elfe as occafion and neceffitie requires , which hee
muft caufe his Sergeant maior to diftribute amongft his
bands, that his fouldiers be not exacted on the prife. The
like diuifion he muft caufe him to make by money it felfe,
but neuer more then that which refts as due to them , as
many very malicioufly haue accuftomed to doe , making
merchandife thereof to the loffe and ruine of their fouldiers: towards whom they are bound continually to
procure manifeft commoditie and profit. The like is to
be obferued in all other things neceffarie and conformable to this before faid , without felling of furniture to
them of exceffiue prife, for nothing is more difhonoura-
ble or more miferable, then to extort vpon fouldiers.

S   It

It is very requisite that hee examine the election and choise, that euery Captaine hath made of his Officers in euery band, and whether they doe thorowly possesse or approach very neere to the perfit experience they ought to doe, of whom and not otherwise he shall like and allow. Note that these aduertisements, make manifest apparence, and sets forth to the view of the world, the inward valour of the Conductour and Collonell: for if he neglect these obseruations, the contrarie doth easily ensue. I iudge it a thing not out of square, but rather most expedient that the one halfe of the Caualliers of the choise squadre should be Hargabusiers on horse-backe, specially when warres be made in large and open countries, or else howsoeuer it be situate: for being men of valour, they may both on horsbacke and foote doe great seruice, as often hath beene tried by manifest experience in our time, specially in the late warres of *Flaunders*, vnder my Collonell the Baron of *Sheueran*, in seruice of *Don Iohn* of *Austria*, and the Prince of *Parma*, where I being of the number of the Gentlemen of his owne band, haue seene daily excellent good seruice done by them, as well by discouering the enemies ambuscades, as to draw them into the danger of our footemen. And likewise in the speedy taking and keeping a passage of importance, in winning aduertisements and the watchword from the enemy, in taking Prisoners, in breaking the way for free passage, in clearing and beating the highwaies, and scouring them free from the enemie and Freebooters, in making roades, courses and incursions, in discouering the Countrey and taking view thereof like to light horsemen, specially in the absence of the Cauallery of the campe. And therefore I conclude that they shall

be

be found to be a knot and kinde of neceſſary ſouldiers, prouided that they be practiſed, and aboue all full of valour and aſpiring mindes, and not to be common ſouldiers, taken at vnawares out of ordinary bands of footmen, neither ſuch as carry a dull, baſe and abiect minde or diſpoſition.

If the Colonell had the authority to be able to keepe together a band with a Standerd or Guidon, & a trumpet to them, they would doe ſinguiar good ſeruice, which neuertheleſſe when ſeruice on foote did call them forth, might deliuer vp their horſes, lances, and hargabuſhes with fire-lockes vnto their ſeruants, kept and maintained for that purpoſe, and enter into ranke or battaile amongſt the reſt of the Caualliers ſquadre, and ſo ſhould the ordinarie and common cuſtome of hauing horſes amongſt priuate ſouldiers be auoided, ſaue ſuch as are permitted and granted to ſome Officers, as in my former diſcourſes I haue already declared. The which obſeruation ſhall bring to paſſe that the ſouldiers in marching and in other enterpriſes ſhall go together, and be vnited about the Enſigne, which is a thing moſt conuenient and neceſſarie, and ought greatly to be ſhunned, for that horſes by ouerthwart trauerſing are accuſtomed to deface the ſquares, and breake the rankes of the footmens battailes, which truely is very odious and of great diſturbance and diſcommodity: but that which I ſpeake of this extraordinarie band is to be vnderſtood and taken, when there is no ordinarie bands of horſemen ioyned to a Collonells regiment. He ought to take vigilant care that the Gentlemen of his band and Caualliers of his ſquadre, being continually about his perſon doe diligently performe, that which they are appointed of him to doe by commiſ-

ſion

fion or otherwife, and that they make faithfull and true relation to him of euery particular thing, that he may be euer fully informed of all things, and chiefly of that which doth paffe in the watch worthy and neceffary to be noted, as well by day as by night, fince that by going the round, which doth appertaine principally to thefe Caualliers, many things of moment and importance may very well be obferued, being able to execute any of the inferiour offices, and both quickly conceiue and fenfibly vtter any new accident.

The Collonell muft moft carefully with humble courtefie court his Captaine generall, vfe great refpect towards him, obey him, and giue him faithfull counfell: and to the end he may performe this thorow well, hee muft neuer refufe toile or trauell, fince that to take paine about matters of like importance, is agreeable and conuenient to honourable perfonages his equals, whereas eafie delicacie and curiofitie appertaines to women, or other effeminate perfons, who efteeme more of bellycheere, gallant attire and riches, then of the peereleffe prife of valour and vertue, and that prefer a fraile body before an immortall foule.

Some hold opinion that a Collonell hauing to allot out what number of pikes, fhort weapons, and fhot is to be in euery band, that it is farre better to haue but one fort of weapons, fo fhall the Captaine euer accompany his own fouldiers, whereas otherwife they being diffeuered in a ftand-battaile, he muft either lofe the company of his fhot or pikes, the one of them being committed to a Second, and the fhort weapons to a Third, which doth nothing fo much encourage the Souldier, as to fee his Captaine companion of his perils, and the contrarie no leffe
                                                                    difmaieth

difmaieth him : but for that foughten fields chance feldome in our time, I ceafe to wade further therein , onely aduertifing that amongft the reft of his fouldiers, the armed pikes muft be gently vfed, fhewing them a cheerefull and good countenance, who muft bee chofen men, very hardy and valiant.

He muft procure that his Officers diligently performe his commiffions , and that faithfully they make relation of euery particular thing, that he may be enformed of all, and efpecially that which happens inwards , as well in the day as in the night, for they going in circuit, as appertaines vnto them, may well perceiue what chanceth of any great importance. So that by obferuing thefe aduertifements, the induftrie of the Leader doth appeare, whereas not being well looked vnto great ruine doth arife.

To conclude, when his regiment is difcharged, either at the end of the warres or otherwife, hee ought to take care that he in any wife procure, that they may bee conducted wholy together, and afterwards difband them in fuch a place, as from thence euery fouldier may eafily and without feare tranfport himfelfe into his owne countrie, and if it be poffible , hauing his health , his armes, and his apparell entire : for otherwife if fouldiers be diffeuered in far countries, they fuffer great inconuenience, in hard and difficile paffages , in victuals and lodgings, the which doth caufe their deftruction, the difcredite and difhonour of their Conductour, and is a great blot in the fame of our nation, as thofe that haue feene *Holland* and the *Low-countries* can witnes : wherfore it is a thing to be reformed for the increafe of our credite and old naturall valour.

S 3 THE

THE
THIRD BOOKE
OF MILITARY
Directions:

*Contayning the exercise of Trayning or
Drilling: and also the manner of arming both Pike
and Musket, according to the custome allowed
in these dayes within this Realme of
England, with certaine other
Observations.*

CHAP. I.

First for the arming of a Pike-man.

T is necessarie that his corslet and gor-
get be fit for his body, as also that his
Tasses and powdrels or arme-pipes be
large and sutable, all these to be strong-
ly buckled and riueted, well oyled and
bright, then a murren or head-peece
well lined, and fringed, agreable to the same: then a
straight pike of a middle size, of 15 foot of length, with
a sharpe iron pike or point at the end, of the right Spanish
fashion, well oyled and bright.

Then

Then that he haue a good back fword with an Irifh basket hilt, and hanged in a ftrong belt.

Note that all Pikes of the fame company ought to be of one length, otherwife if they difagree, they will be vncomely, and feeme to the beholders like vnto Organpipes, which be of different lengths. Moreouer, they are very vnprofitable for feruice, for they will greatly trouble each other, and efpecially the huge and long pikes, and therefore are to be refufed. Likewife a fhort pike is not good in a maine fquare, neither in campe or battell, except it be in ftrait and narrow places.

Secondly, for the ordering and arming of a Musketeere.

IT is conuenient that the barrell or canon of his peece be in length foure foote at the leaft, cleane and found, with a ftraight and right bore, hauing a clofe ftocke and well ioyned thereunto, of a right Spanifh making: Then that the cocke of his peece be fwift and well oyled, bearing a true deliuerance to the middeft of the pan, the touch-hole neither too great or too narrow, the pan clofe, the eye-fight true, and then hauing a ftrong breech-peece, looke that all thefe inftruments be well fcrued, and efpecially the breech-peece: A charging rod or fticke of a meete length to the barrell of the peece, the fame to haue a worme or a fcowrer at the one end, the other end thereof tipped with a horne.

Then fore-fee that he haue a Bandeleere with 16 or 18 chargers or mates at the leaft, hanged thereunto, with ftrong laces, with a priming charger or mate, and alfo a bullet bag and priming wyre: then a Reft of a fit fize and

and length breaſt or chin high, with a trayle lace faſtned thereat, togither with a head-peece or murren, and ſword in all points prouided as is aforeſaid.

Chap. II.

The Office of the Muſter-Maſter, both neceſſarie and pro-
fitable, when a Prince or his Generall haue
diuers Regiments of feuerall Nati-
ons vnder pay.

THe Muſter-Maſter alſo may be accounted an Officer as it were dependant on the Treaſurer, for that his dutie is nothing elſe, but by often reviewing of the bands, to ſee how euery Captaines band is furniſhed (according to my former directions for the arming both pike and musket) noting the defaults from time to time, and the ſupplies; and thereof to make a perfect booke, exhibiting the ſame at the pay day to the Treaſurer, that allowance may be made to the Colonels and Captaines accordingly. When he firſt takes the view and muſter of any band, he muſt not onely write downe the name of the ſoldier and his weapon, but alſo of what Country he is, the townes name where he was borne, and his fathers name, and what yeeres he is of: and finally ſhall take ſpeciall care to ſet downe, ſome ſpeciall marke or cicatrice vpon his face, togither with the colour of his haire and beard: to the intent, his Prince be not charged with paying of dead payes, to ſuch as be hyred but for that day, as many Captaines vſe to fill their purſes with vnlawfull gaines.

Chap. III.

Chap. III.

A Rule to set Souldiers in aray.

THe Footmen being assembled at the place where they are to be set in aray: First, you must foresee, that the ground be fit and capable for the purpose, that the aray may commodiously turne to the right or left hand, as much as may be neuerthelesse, according to the number of soldiers you haue, you are to proceed in this sort as followeth.

First, to wit that all the soldiers of a band of footmen are bound by the law of Armes, forthwith and as soone as they shall heare the Drum beat a Call to repaire to the Colours, vnder paine &c. except that sicknes be the cause thereof; or that hauing a licence or forelose they may thereby excuse themselues. But to returne: you are to begin in this order following: First, you are to draw the pikes by themselues on the one side, togither with the Ensigne: and vpon the other side all the musketiers, somewhat aloose distant from the pikes, beginning to make the musketiers march so many in a ranke as you list, parting them neuerthelesse according to their number: you may put them from 3 to 12 in a ranke; for it is not often seene that more than 11 is put in a ranke, how great soeuer the number of the footmen be: neither in troth ought they to be any more than 11 in a ranke: for when they passe 11 or 12 they are not to be accounted an array, but rather a battaile: I haue omitted to write herein of the placing of my officers belonging to a company of footmen, you shall finde it plainely set downe in the march, and at the beginning of the exercise of

T   training:

training: so to returne, hauing then placed the number of musketiers you shall thinke good of to be in a ranke, you shall cause them to march in good proportion, sending forth one ranke after an other; the Sargeant standing still on the one side, causing them to passe before him, iudging by the eye-sight from Ranke to Ranke of all the soldiers, one by one, whether they be right in line, obseruing true distance: and also that they carry their Armes in warlike order; for this is the beauty of an aray. Moreouer the Sargeant hauing speciall respect to accommodate and place at the head of the array, the Gentlemen of the company, and also the Corporals which carry muskets; placing next vnto them the best men, and the best furnished soldiers; and placing also at the Reare of the battell your best men, and the rest of your best armed; to the intent the aray may shew the better: forasmuch as when they are diuided into aray, the musketiers from the pikemen, and that they turne their faces; then the backe part or Reare is made the front: therefore the Reare ought to be as well furnished as the front, as I haue said before in the dutie of a Sargeant: the which if you desire to doe, it is necessarie you put in the midst of the Rankes the weakest and worst furnished; aduertising the Sargeant that the soldiers are best furnished, when they haue all sorts of Armes and furniture that be necessarie for them: and there appertaines to a musketier good match, fire-cole, powder and bullet, and moreouer *l'assino.* And this is to be obserued with all speed and diligence that the time or occasion doth carry, and the suspition of the enemy doth import.

Here

Here next is demonstrated the distance observed betwixt Ranke and Ranke, man and man, both in marching, and also in maine battaile.

FIrst both pikes and muskets are to be ordered into files of 10 deepe, the musketiers in marching are sometimes placed in the front, sometimes in the front and sometimes in the Reare of the pikes, but most commonly being in single aray they are to march both in the Front and Reare : In maine battell the soldiers are placed sometimes in the right flanke, sometimes in both the flankes ; and sometimes it will be commanded that they be brought in the Front of the battaile, and also in the Reare.

In exercising the motions there are two distances to be kept.

The first is when euery one is distant from his fellow 6 foote square ; that is, in File and Ranke 6 foote.

The second is when euery soldier is 3 foote distant one from another, as well in File as in Ranke : And in respect the measure of such distances cannot alwaies be taken euenly by the racke of the eye ; the distance of 6 foote betweene the files is measured, when the soldiers stretching out their armes, doe touch one anothers hands : and betwixt the Rankes, when that the ends of their pikes come very neere to the hams of them that march before them : And the distance of 3 foot betwixt the Files is when their elbowes touch one another : and betwixt their Rankes when they come to touch the ends of one anothers Rapiers or swords. In marching in the

T 2   field

field the diftance of 3 foote from File to File is kept, and of 6 foote from Ranke to Ranke, when the foldiers order themfelues in battell; and alfo when they march towards the enemie, the diftance of 3 foote both in File and Ranke is to be obferued. And likewife in conuerfion or wheeling. The musketiers making ready to fhoote by rankes keepe the fame diftance of 3 foote, but going to skirmifh they goe *a la difabande*, that is, out of order.

There is alfo vfed another order of diftance; which is feldome obferued but for to receiue the enemie with a firme ftand, and ferueth for the pikes onely: for the musketiers cannot ftand fo clofe in files, becaufe they muft haue their armes at liberty, and that is, when euery diftance from file to file is a foote and a halfe, and 3 foote from Ranke to Ranke: and this laft diftance is thus commanded: *Clofe your felues throughly.* But it is not to be taught the foldiers: for that when neceffitie fhall require it, they will clofe themfelues too much of their owne accord without command.

How Pikes are to be raifed vp and abafed in clofing and opening of a battaile.

I Will not omit to put in memorie vnto them that know not of the particulars of thofe things and order that are required in making a battell of footmen. Therefore thofe which would make a battell of footmen, muft be aduertifed that in fhutting vp the faid battell, the ranks of pikes as well armed as vnarmed, muft not raife vp confufedly, but with order; that is, when the Sargeant maior, Captaine, or Lieutenant fhall fay:

Raife

Raife or right vp your Pikes,

then it is requifite that the firft and formoft Ranke muft begin to raife vp it felfe: and that the fecond doe not moue to raife vp it felfe till the firft be raifed vp: and fo the third and fourth: the fame order is to be obferued in all the other Rankes, from one Ranke to an other.

The like Rule is to be obferued by them in laying downe of their pikes vpon their fhoulders: for fo much as Ranke by Ranke, in order and without confufion they ought to let fall their pikes; appointing the firft Ranke to fall after the fecond, the third after the fourth: and fo is all the reft of the Rankes to follow the fame order, till the hindermoft Ranke of all: And by obferuing that order, they cannot commit diforder, but rather make a gallant fhew, and preuent many confufions.

How Pikes are to be carried in aray, march, or battell,
with alfo other neceffarie notes.

THofe that are appointed to carry pikes in array of Rankes or battell, muft know that pikes amongft all other weapons that belong to foldiers is of greateft honor and credit: And truely whofoeuer doth carry and manage the fame weapon well, and with good grace, doth make a very beautifull and pleafant fhew to the beholders; and chiefly when it is caried with a good grace, as I haue faid before, and with *il combedo alto.* And as touching the obferuation of fhouldring of pikes, to wit, that there is a new order obferued in the Low Countries now of late; the Commanders there will haue the pikes to be carried vpon the right fhoulder, and not to remoue or change to the left fhoulder at all.

Note

Note alfo that the Pike-man doe march then with a good grace holding vp his head gallantly : his pace full of grauitie and eftate, and fuch as is fit for his perfon : And let his body be ftraight and as much vpright as is poffible : And that which moft imports is that they haue alwaies their eyes vpon their companions which are in ranke with them ; and before them : going iuft one with the other : and keeping perfit diftance without committing error in the leaft pace or ftep : and euery pace and motion with one accord and confent ; they ought to make at one inftant time : And in this fort all the rankes intirely are to march fometimes foftly fometimes faft according to the ftrokes of the drumme : the heele and the tippe of their pikes would be equally holden : both of length and height as neere as is poffible : to auoid that they fall not out to be feeme by bearing them otherwife like vnto Organ-pipes fome long fome fhort. The meafure and propertie thereof : to hold the heele of the pike is this ; it is neceffarie for him to haue an eie to the ranke that doth march before him : and fo carrie the Butt-end or heele of his pike that it may be iuft ouer againft the ioynt of the hamme of the fouldier that in march fhall be ftraight before him : And fo euery one from hand to hand muft obferue the proportion of that height : And that is, right behind vpon the ioynt of the knee : for by doing fo they cannot commit errour ; carying in their march that legge that is vnder that arme that fuftaines and caries the Pike of iuft and euen proportion : by mouing their pace right-vnder the ftaffe of the pike : going in their march as I haue faid before : iuft and euen with a ftately and fumptuous pace, for by doing fo they fhall be efteemed, honoured and commended of all the Lookers

on,

on, and they will take wonderfull delight to behold them
march in that order: And whereas I haue said before that
the Souldiers should march forward with one consent:
I meane not onely that the Pike men ought to obserue
that order: but also that the musketeares are to follow
the same rule of order: because that the whole company
must be ready to march forward at one instant time obseruing the true strokes or battery of the drumme, which
actiue obseruation may well be compared to a Dancer;
for the one by hearing his musicke is prepared to tread
the measure answerable to the time : And the other by
hearing the warlike and comfortable stroke of the drum:
is ready to aduance his pace and march forward.

The Officer is to pace towards his people, so to giue
the word, and so to lead march, and also obseruing the
strokes of the drum, the first ranke being the file leaders
it to follow their Leader : The second ranke euery one
to follow his pile-leader also: The third, fourth and fift
rankes; and so the rest with one consent.

I hold it therefore both conuenient and needfull for all
men that follow the warres, to learne all the warlike
sounds that the Drummer beates, as the call, the march,
to draw vp maine-battell, the charge, the retire, to troupe,
to wheele about which is also a charge, then and lastly
the diana. And whereas euery nation doe differ the one
from the other in the batterie of their drummes, and
chiefly in the sound of their march euery nation or Pro-
uince doe also differ in the marke of their colours, for that
they beare in their colours the proper Armes or Scutchi-
on of the Nation vnder which they doe serue. But to
returne, let a souldier be diligent to learne, as I said before, the strokes of the drumme : And chiefly to vnder-

stand

stand the vsuall strokes of march which the drumme beat in the regiment wherein he beareth armes : he must also take notice of the markes that are vpon the colours; especially of the Ensigne which hee serueth vnder, the knowledge whereof may serue his turne so well that it may saue his life, for by night being in fight with the enemie, and being also ignorant of the sound of drumme, he may aswell fall into the hands of his enemies as otherwise, which may cost him his life : Then as touching his Ensigne the souldier being scattered from his company in marching, or otherwise in fight, and if it be by daylight he may perceiue his owne colours farre off. To wit, that both drummes and fifes were first inuented by the *Switzers*, wherewith they will euen liue and die in all manner of fight. The *Almaines* also inuented a pipe which is called by them *Schalmeyen*. Some nations when they doe fight a pitched field by reason of the tumult, and rumour that will grow amongst the souldiers, they haue trumpets to giue the charge, which yeeldeth great comfort to the souldiers in regard that they heare the eccho and sound of the trumpets so plaine, that in all distresse they doe not onely keep together, but also know their charge. Therefore in forraine Countries the footmen are as well acquainted in all points of warre which the said trumpets doe vse to sound that they know their charge euen as well as horsemen doe. But to returne to the matter aforesaid : the *Turke* when he doth either expect the charge giuen him by his enemies, or when he will giue a charge &c. it will bee commanded that a Drummer shall ride from ranke to ranke to giue the souldiers notice by a soft sound : And as touching marching, it is to be vnderstood that some kinde of march is a right

induction

induction ; other fome a deduction on the right or left hand ; and that in fingle, double, treble, or quadruple fided battell : in a fingle when one enemie is feared ; in a double when two ; in a treble when three ; and in a quadruble when the enemie purpofeth to inuade on all fides : Therefore the march is vndertaken fometimes in a fingle challenge, and fometimes in a twofold challenge, or elfe in a threefold challenge, or in a fourefold challenge. The fouldiers, both Pikemen and Musketeares are to be diuided into companies, and euery company is to confift halfe of pikes, and halfe of musketeares.

The companies happen and fall out fometimes to be more in number, and fometimes leffe ; fome extend to 100. men, fome 200. fome 300. fome 400. and fo forth till 800 men or more. Euery company ought to haue thefe Officers following: a Captaine, a Lieutenant, an Enfigne, two Sergeants, three Corporalls, two Drums; but by the opinion of many worthy fouldiers, euery hundreth men ought to haue a Drumme ; the reafon whereof I omit to fpeake thereof in this place, and returne to the matter : it will be needfull for a Captaine to haue in his company for neceffarie vfes a Clarke, a Surgeon, and a Prouoft. Companies are drawne into Regiments, and the Regiments are euer to be commanded by Coronells : Regiments doe fometimes likewife differ in the number of companies, fome confift of 6. fome of 7. fome of 8. or 10. fome 15. &c. In the ordering, and managing of euery regiment is to be required a Coronell &c.

V

Certaine

*Certaine words to be vfed of the Officers
that traine.*

WHen any Officer determines to exercife his companie to traine, or drill them, hee muft caft them
into a ring, the double or fingle biffa, the Romane S or
fuch like neceffarie forme, and vfe thefe or the like words
as heare followeth : My louing friends, fellowes, and
companions in armes, we be gathered together for the
feruice of God, his holy Church, our Prince and Countrey ; and for that none through ignorance fhall perifh or
runne in danger of the Lawes of the Field, you fhall
from time to time, by me or other Officers of the Band
be inftructed by words or deedes in fuch fort, and points,
as to your calling and the neceffitie of feruice fhall require, the which you muft diligently obferue, and follow, though the fame fhall feeme vnto you many times,
both dangerous and painefull : alfo if any of you, my fellowes fhall finde an occafion conuenient to declare to
me, or any other Officer, his minde and opinion in any
thing beneficiall touching feruice, wee fhall diligently
heare, and gratifie the party the double value thereof;
and God willing Equitie and Iuftice fhall bee miniftred;
alfo regard that all Souldiers know, and obey their Officers in their place, according to their calling.

The

The firſt thing of moment in the motion of a Company is how they ſhould orderly march, and how their Officers ſhould be rightly placed, the which I haue demonſtrated in the figure on the other ſide, according as it is practiſed in the *Low-countries*, the ſchoole of warre: Firſt the Captaine, marcheth in the Front, and leades the company, whoſe place is marked with C: which is ſix foote diſtant before the firſt diuiſion of muketeares. The Lieutenant is to march in the Reare of the ſecond diuiſion of Musketeares, marked with L: ſix foot diſtant behind the ſame. The Enſigne is to march with the colours ſix foot behind the firſt diuiſion of Musketeares, and ſix foot before the firſt diuiſion of pikes, marked with the letter E. The eldeſt Sergeant is to march ſix foot behind the firſt diuiſion of pikes, and ſix foot before the ſecond diuiſion of pikes, marked with S. 1. The ſecond Sergeant is to march ſix foote behind the ſecond diuiſion of pikes, and ſix foot before the ſecond diuiſion of musketeares, marked with S. 2. the drummes beate betweene the third and fourth rankes, marked with D: The chiefeſt beates in the firſt diuiſion of pikes; The ſecond in the firſt diuiſion of musketeares; And the third drumme beates in the ſecond diuiſion of musketeares: The pikes and muskets march ſix foot in file, and three in ranke, euery diuiſion conſiſts of ten rankes and fiue files, all which is made plaine in the next figure following.

The order

C

The order how a Companie should march.

MMMMM Leaders.
MMMMM
MMMMM
D
MMMMM
MMMMM
MMMMM
MMMMM
MMMMM
MMMMM
MMMMM Bringers vp.

First diuision of Musketieres.

E

PPPPP Leaders.
PPPPP
PPPPP
D
PPPPP
PPPPP
PPPPP
PPPPP
PPPPP
PPPPP
PPPPP Bringers vp.

First diuision of Pikes.

S 1.

PPPPP Leaders.
PPPPP
PPPPP
PPPPP
PPPPP
PPPPP
PPPPP
PPPPP
PPPPP

Second diuision of Pikes.

AFter that the company hath marched in such order as aforesaid in the former figure, then the first diuisiō of shot (when they are come to the place where they should exercise, traine, or drill) makes a stand; and the first diuision of the pikes marcheth vp to the front with them, on the left hand: Then the second diuision of the pikes marcheth vp to the front with the first diuision of pikes, on the left hand of them also: lastly, the second diuision of musketiers marcheth vp on the left hand of the second diuision of pikes: which done they are commanded to *stand right in their files*, and *right in their rankes*, *at 6 foote distance*, and commanded, *silence*, that euery one may heare the words of command, and be ready to execute the same. The figure on the other side *pag.* 149 sheweth the forme and station of the company, all things performed as aforesaid: note the distance is reckoned from the middle part of a man.

Front

left flanke

M M M M M P P P P P P P P P P M M M M M
M M M M M P P P P P P P P P P M M M M M
M M M M M P P P P P P P P P P M M M M M
M M M M M P P P P P P P P P P M M M M M
M M M M M P P P P P P P P P P M M M M M
M M M M M P P P P P P P P P P M M M M M
M M M M M P P P P P P P P P P M M M M M
M M M M M P P P P P P P P P P M M M M M
M M M M M P P P P P P P P P P M M M M M
M M M M M P P P P P P P P P P M M M M M

right flanke

Reare

To the right hand.

The Company ſtanding right in their files and rankes, at ſix foote diſtance (as in the figure before) vnto which the Captaine hath an eye in the front, and the Lieutenant in the Reare, and the Sargeants in the flanks ; the Sargeants hauing an eare to the Captaine are ready to informe the company what he commands : then the Captaine commands them to *turne to the right hand* ; and then they moue all togither, keeping their left foote fixed, and mouing with the right foote onely ; and hauing performed it ; the front is where the right hand flanke was; as in the figure pag. 151 is plainely demonſtrated.

Note that in or at their facing to any quarter, the pikes are (to auoide wearineſſe) ordered ; and the muskets ſhouldred for eaſe and fitneſſe. The reaſon of this motion is to make the company perfect to be ſodainely prepared for a charge in the right hand, flanke or wing.

M M M M M P P P P P P P P P M M M M M
M M M M M P P P P P P P P P M M M M M
M M M M M P P P P P P P P P M M M M M
M M M M M P P P P P P P P P M M M M M
M M M M M P P P P P P P P P M M M M M
M M M M M P P P P P P P P P M M M M M
M M M M M P P P P P P P P P M M M M M
M M M M M P P P P P P P P P M M M M M
M M M M M P P P P P P P P P M M M M M
M M M M M P P P P P P P P P M M M M M

As you were.

HAuing ftood a while according to the forme in the former figure, the Captaine commands , *As you were*, and then they moue all towards the lett hand, till their faces are turned to the firft Front, according to the demonftration, pag. 153.

M M M M M P P P P P P P P P P P M M M M M

M M M M M P P P P P P P P P P P M M M M M

M M M M M P P P P P P P P P P P M M M M M

M M M M M P P P P P P P P P P P M M M M M

M M M M M P P P P P P P P P P P M M M M M

M M M M M P P P P P P P P P P P M M M M M

M M M M M P P P P P P P P P P P M M M M M

M M M M M P P P P P P P P P P P M M M M M

M M M M M P P P P P P P P P P P M M M M M

M M M M M P P P P P P P P P P P M M M M M

X

To the left hand.

BEcaufe the enewie may fometimes charge on the left hand flanke, therfore that you may fodainely be ready to defend your felues, and for diuers other reafons this motion is vfed, to *turne to the left hand,* which is done by mouing the right foot, the left foot ftanding ftill till your faces front towards the left hand flanke, according to the demonftration, pag. 1 5 5.

M M M M M M P P P P P P P P P P M M M M
M M M M M M P P P P P P P P P P M M M M
M M M M M M P P P P P P P P P P M M M M
M M M M M M P P P P P P P P P P M M M M
M M M M M M P P P P P P P P P P M M M M
M M M M M M P P P P P P P P P P M M M M
M M M M M M P P P P P P P P P P M M M M
M M M M M M P P P P P P P P P P M M M M
M M M M M M P P P P P P P P P P M M M M

As you were.

THen hauing performed the aforefaid motion, the Captaine Commands ; *As you were :* and then they moue all towards the right hand, till they are turned to the firft Front, according to the demonftration *pag.* 157.

M M M M M P P P P P P P P P M M M M M
M M M M M P P P P P P P P P M M M M M
M M M M M P P P P P P P P P M M M M M
M M M M M P P P P P P P P P M M M M M
M M M M M P P P P P P P P P M M M M M
M M M M M P P P P P P P P P M M M M M
M M M M M P P P P P P P P P M M M M M
M M M M M P P P P P P P P P M M M M M
M M M M M P P P P P P P P P M M M M M
M M M M M P P P P P P P P P M M M M M

X 3   *To*

To the right hand about.

BEcaufe there may be a charge giuen in the Reare, therefore is this Motion to be practifed, to turne towards the right hand (the left foote remaining fixed) till your faces front to that Quarter which was before the Reare ; and then will they be ready to receiue the Enemie and defend themfelues : this forme is demonftrated in the next fide, marked with the number of 159.

M

W W W W W d d d d d d d d d d W W W W W
W W W W W d d d d d d d d d d W W W W W
W W W W W d d d d d d d d d d W W W W W
W W W W W d d d d d d d d d d W W W W W
W W W W W d d d d d d d d d d W W W W W
W W W W W d d d d d d d d p W W W W W
W W W W W d d d d d d d d d W W W W W
W W W W W d d d d d d d d d W W W W W
W W W W W d d d d p p p p p W W W W W
W W W W W d d d d p p p p p W W W W W

Hauing

To the left hand as you were.

HAuing performed the former Motion, the Captaine commands them, *To the left hand as you were;* and then they moue all towards the left hand, the left foot remaining fixed, vntill their faces are turned to the former front: according to that of *pag.* 161.

M M M M M P P P P P P P P P P M M M M M
M M M M M P P P P P P P P P P M M M M M
M M M M M P P P P P P P P P P M M M M M
M M M M M P P P P P P P P P P M M M M M
M M M M M P P P P P P P P P P M M M M M
M M M M M P P P P P P P P P P M M M M M
M M M M M P P P P P P P P P P M M M M M
M M M M M P P P P P P P P P P M M M M M
M M M M M P P P P P P P P P P M M M M M
M M M M M P P P P P P P P P P M M M M M

Y   To

To the left hand about.

BEcaufe it is fometimes more conuenient to turne to
the left hand, then to the right, therefore this Motion
is alfo vfed ; which is to turne towards the left hand , till
their faces front to the Reare : according to the figure
in the *pag.* 163.

M M M M M d d d d d d d d d d M M M M M
M M M M M d d d d d d d d d d M M M M M
M M M M M d d d d d d d d d d M M M M M
M M M M M d d d d d d d d d d M M M M M
M M M M M d d d d d d d d d d M M M M M
M M M M M d d d d d d d d d d M M M M M
M M M M M d d d d d d d d d d M M M M M
M M M M M d d d d d d d d d d M M M M M
M M M M M d d d d d d d d d d M M M M M
M M M M M d d d d d d d d d d M M M M M

To the right hand as you were.

HAuing performed the former Motion, the Captaine cōmands them, *To the right hand as you were;*
and then they turne all towards the right hand, vntill
their faces are towards the firſt Front, as in the figure
pag. 165.

M M M M M P P P P P P P P P P M M M M M
M M M M M P P P P P P P P P P M M M M M
M M M M M P P P P P P P P P P M M M M M
M M M M M P P P P P P P P P P M M M M M
M M M M M P P P P P P P P P P M M M M M
M M M M M P P P P P P P P P P M M M M M
M M M M M P P P P P P P P P P M M M M M
M M M M M P P P P P P P P P P M M M M M
M M M M M P P P P P P P P P P M M M M M
M M M M M P P P P P P P P P P M M M M M

Y 3

To the right hand double your Ranckes.

BEcaufe there will be an occafion fometimes to ftren-
gthen the Front ; it may one way be done thus:when
all in the fecond Rancke march vp into the firft Rancke,
to the right or left hand, according to the command (as
here to the right hand) and all in the fourth Rancke
march vp into the third, and fo of the reft, as in the Example or Figure,pag.167. Where you may perceiue by
the letters marked with a Starre, that the motion is to the
right hand: and the Starres in the fecond, fourth, fixt,
eighth,and tenth Ranckes fhew the places from whence
they moued: and the figures in the left flank demonftra-
ting the number of your Ranckes which did moue,being
ten Ranckes,as you may perceiue thereby.

1 m m m m m m m m m m p p p p p p p p p p p p p p p p p p p m m m m m m m m m m
     *

2 *

3 m m m m m m m m m m p p p p p p p p p p p p p p p p p p p m m m m m m m m m m
     *

4 *

5 m m m m m m m m m m p p p p p p p p p p p p p p p p p p p m m m m m m m m m m
     *

6 *

7 m m m m m m m m m m p p p p p p p p p p p p p p p p p p p m m m m m m m m m m
     *

8 *

9 m m m m m m m m m m p p p p p p p p p p p p p p p p p p p m m m m m m m m m m
     *

10 *

Ranckes as you were.

Auing performed the former motion, the Captaine
commands, *Ranckes as you were*; and then euery
one marcheth into his owne place, all at one inftant, and
fo are againe like the forme in the figure, pag.169.

```
M *M M M M M P P P P P P P P P P M M M M M M
M M M M M M P P P P P P P P P P M M M M M M
M *M M M M M P P P P P P P P P P M M M M M M
M M M M M M P P P P P P P P P P M M M M M M
M *M M M M M P P P P P P P P P P M M M M M M
M M M M M M P P P P P P P P P P M M M M M M
M *M M M M M P P P P P P P P P P M M M M M M
M M M M M M P P P P P P P P P P M M M M M M
M *M M M M M P P P P P P P P P P M M M M M M
M M M M M M P P P P P P P P P P M M M M M M
```

Z

To the left hand double your Ranckes.

THis Motion differeth nothing in effect from that
pag. 167. but that there thofe that doubled, did it to
the right hand of their Leaders, and here they do it to the
left hand: which is plaine by the Starres in the Figure,
pag. 171.

1   m m m m m m m m m p p p p p p p p p p p p p p p p p p m m m m m m m m m m m
     ✶

2   ✶

3   m m m m m m m m m m m p p p p p p p p p p p p p p p p p p m m m m m m m m m m m m
     ✶

4   ✶

5   m m m m m m m m m m m m p p p p p p p p p p p p p p p p p p m m m m m m m m m m m
     ✶

6   ✶

7   m m m m m m m m m m m p p p p p p p p p p p p p p p p p p m m m m m m m m m m m
     ✶

8   ✶

9   m m m m m m m m m m p p p p p p p p p p p p p p p p p p p m m m m m m m m m m m
     ✶

10   ✶

Z 2

Ranckes as you were.

THe former motion performed, the Captaine commands, *Ranckes as you were*; and then euery one
that doubled, marcheth into his owne place or Rancke,
and fo are in forme againe, according to the figure,
pag. 173.

```
*M M M M M P P P P P P P P P P PM M M M M
 M M M M M P P P P P P P P P PM M M M M
*M M M M M P P P P P P P P P P PM M M M M
 M M M M M P P P P P P P P P PM M M M M
*M M M M M P P P P P P P P P P PM M M M M
 M M M M M P P P P P P P P P P PM M M M M
*M M M M M P P P P P P P P P P PM M M M M
 M M M M M P P P P P P P P P PM M M M M
*M M M M M P P P P P P P P P PM M M M M
 M M M M M P P P P P P P P P PM M M M M
```

Z 3   Becaufe

BEcaufe that there was an odde file of musketeares, in either flanke and wing of my former figures, and being defirous to make the double files perfit without intermixing the pikes with the fhot, I was forced therefore to change the forme of the Company, and to place all the Musketeares in the Right hand flanke of the Pikes, according to the demonftration in the other fide marked with the number of 175.

Note then to alter the forme of the former ftation, and to bring the Company into the forme, fet downe in the other fide, (as I faid before) you are to doe as followeth. Firft you are to lead forth the Right wing of fhot, then the firft diuifion of Pikes, which be in the right hand flanke of the fecond diuifion of pikes, and march with them to ftand iuft againft the firft diuifion of musketeares, on the left hand of them, leauing a fpace to place the fecond diuifion of fhot betweene them both; then you are to march vp with the fecond diuifion of Pikes to ftand on the left hand of the firft diuifion of Pikes : Laftly, the fecond diuifion of Musketeaies, marcheth vp to ftand on the left hand of the firft diuifion of Musketeares, which will be on the right hand of the firft diuifion of Pikes: which done, they are commanded to ftand right in their Files, and right in their Rankes, at fix foot diftance, and commanded filence, that fo euery one may heare the words of Command, and to be ready to execute the fame. &c.

Front.

P P P P P P P P P P M M M M M M M M M M
P P P P P P P P P P M M M M M M M M M M
P P P P P P P P P P M M M M M M M M M M
P P P P P P P P P P M M M M M M M M M M
P P P P P P P P P P M M M M M M M M M M
P P P P P P P P P P M M M M M M M M M M
P P P P P P P P P P M M M M M M M M M M
P P P P P P P P P P M M M M M M M M M M
P P P P P P P P P P M M M M M M M M M M
P P P P P P P P P P M M M M M M M M M M

Reare.

To

To the right hand double your files.

BEcaufe there may be occafion of ftrengthning the Flankes, as alfo for other purpofes, thefe words of Command are vfed, *To the right hand double your Files*; which is thus performed: All the fecond file, from the right hand, march euery one behinde his fide-man, into the firft (or right hand) File, and fo the fourth File into the third, and the fixt into the fift, &c. which is done of all at one inftant after the command is giuen. The order whereof is plainely demonftrated in the Figure marked with 177. In which you may perceiue by the Starres, from, and to what place each man marcheth. The Stars are onely fet downe in the firft and fecond Files, but you are to vnderftand the fame order in the third and fourth Files, and fo of all the reft. &c.

20	19	18	17	16	15	14	13	12	11	10	9	8	7	6	5	4	3	2	1
	P		P		P		P		P		M		M		M		M	*	M
	P		P		P		P		P		M		M		M		M	*	M
	P		P		P		P		P		M		M		M		M	*	M
	P		P		P		P		P		M		M		M		M	*	M
	P		P		P		P		P		M		M		M		M	*	M
	P		P		P		P		P		M		M		M		M	*	M
	P		P		P		P		P		M		M		M		M	*	M
	P		P		P		P		P		M		M		M		M	*	M
	P		P		P		P		P		M		M		M		M	*	M
	P		P		P		P		P		M		M		M		M	*	M
	P		P		P		P		P		M		M		M		M	*	M
	P		P		P		P		P		M		M		M		M	*	M
	P		P		P		P		P		M		M		M		M	*	M
	P		P		P		P		P		M		M		M		M	*	M
	P		P		P		P		P		M		M		M		M	*	M
	P		P		P		P		P		M		M		M		M	*	M
	P		P		P		P		P		M		M		M		M	*	M
	P		P		P		P		P		M		M		M		M	*	M
	P		P		P		P		P		M		M		M		M	*	M
	P		P		P		P		P		M		M		M		M	*	M

A a

Files as you were.

HAuing performed the former Motion, the Captaine commands them, *Files as you were* ; and then all thofe which doubled, returne vnto their owne proper places: the which is plainely demonftrated in the Figure marked with 179. by the Starres in the firft and fecond Files, the which order you muft conceiue in the third and fourth, fift and fixt, &c.

```
P  P  P  P  P  P  P  P  P  P  P  M  M  M  M  M  M  M  M  M  M* M
                                                              *
P  P  P  P  P  P  P  P  P  P  P  M  M  M  M  M  M  M  M  M  M* M
                                                              *
P  P  P  P  P  P  P  P  P  P  P  M  M  M  M  M  M  M  M  M  M* M
                                                              *
P  P  P  P  P  P  P  P  P  P  P  M  M  M  M  M  M  M  M  M  M* M
                                                              *
P  P  P  P  P  P  P  P  P  P  P  M  M  M  M  M  M  M  M  M  M* M
                                                              *
P  P  P  P  P  P  P  P  P  P  P  M  M  M  M  M  M  M  M  M  M* M
                                                              *
P  P  P  P  P  P  P  P  P  P  P  M  M  M  M  M  M  M  M  M  M* M
                                                              *
P  P  P  P  P  P  P  P  P  P  P  M  M  M  M  M  M  M  M  M  M* M
                                                              *
P  P  P  P  P  P  P  P  P  P  P  M  M  M  M  M  M  M  M  M  M* M
                                                              *
P  P  P  P  P  P  P  P  P  P  P  M  M  M  M  M  M  M  M  M  M* M
                                                              *
```

A 2

To

To the left hand double your files.

THis Motion differeth little from that marked with 177. but that here the Motion is to the left hand, as there it was to the right hand : so that those Files which moued then, stand still now ; and those which stood still then, moue now : all which is so plainly demonstrated by the Starres in the figure marked with 181. that it needs no further explanation.

P	P	P	P	P	M	M	M	M	M	*
P	P	P	P	P	M	M	M	M	M*	
P	P	P	P	P	M	M	M	M	M	*
P	P	P	P	P	M	M	M	M	M*	
P	P	P	P	P	M	M	M	M	M	*
P	P	P	P	P	M	M	M	M	M*	
P	P	P	P	P	M	M	M	M	M	*
P	P	P	P	P	M	M	M	M	M*	
P	P	P	P	P	M	M	M	M	M	*
P	P	P	P	P	M	M	M	M	M*	
P	P	P	P	P	M	M	M	M	M	*
P	P	P	P	P	M	M	M	M	M*	
P	P	P	P	P	M	M	M	M	M	*
P	P	P	P	P	M	M	M	M	M*	
P	P	P	P	P	M	M	M	M	M	*
P	P	P	P	P	M	M	M	M	M*	
P	P	P	P	P	M	M	M	M	M	*
P	P	P	P	P	M	M	M	M	M*	
P	P	P	P	P	M	M	M	M	M	*
P	P	P	P	P	M	M	M	M	M*	

A a 3

Files as you were.

THe former Motion orderly performed, the Captaine commands, *Files as you were*; and then thofe which doubled, returne into their proper places: according as you may plainely vnderftand by the figure pag 183. in which the *Starres* demonftrate both from what place they come, and whither they march.

P P P P P P P P P P M M M M M M M M M M* M
P P P P P P P P P P M M M M M M M M M M* M
P P P P P P P P P P M M M M M M M M M M* M
P P P P P P P P P P M M M M M M M M M M* M
P P P P P P P P P P M M M M M M M M M M* M
P P P P P P P P P P M M M M M M M M M M* M
P P P P P P P P P P M M M M M M M M M M* M
P P P P P P P P P P M M M M M M M M M M* M
P P P P P P P P P P M M M M M M M M M M* M
P P P P P P P P P P M M M M M M M M M M* M

HAuing performed the doubling of Files in all points and orders demonftrated in my figures before this, which was done with the fhot inthe right hand flanke of the pikes: hereafter followeth the exercife in the very fame forme and ftation of the Company where with I began the exercife of training: the which Musketiers are diuided and placed in both the flankes of the pikes, according to the figure in the next fide, pag.185.

```
M M M M M P P P P P P P P P P M M M M M
M M M M M P P P P P P P P P P M M M M M
M M M M M P P P P P P P P P P M M M M M
M M M M M P P P P P P P P P P M M M M M
M M M M M P P P P P P P P P P M M M M M
M M M M M P P P P P P P P P P M M M M M
M M M M M P P P P P P P P P P M M M M M
M M M M M P P P P P P P P P P M M M M M
M M M M M P P P P P P P P P P M M M M M
M M M M M P P P P P P P P P P M M M M M
```

Bb

Halfe Files to the right hand double your Ranckes.

IN the figure, *pag.* 166. was shewed one way how that vpon occasion the Front might be strengthned : here is another forme of strengthning the same ; which requireth two demonstrations or Figures for explanation. In the first marked with D. is shewed the manner of acting this Motion ; and in the second marked with E. is demonstrated the action performed : wherein you may perceiue how the sixt Rancke, or as some improperly call them, *middle men*, doubleth the first Rancke, the seuenth the second Rancke, the eight the third Rancke, the ninth the fourth Rancke, and the tenth the fift Rancke. Note that in performing this motion, the halfe files of Pikes that doubled, aduance their Pikes till they haue doubled, and then order them.

D

mmmmmmmmmmmmmppppppppppppppppppppmmmmmmmmmmm

mmmmmmmmmmmppppppppppppppppppppppmmmmmmmmmmm

mmmmmmmmmmmmppppppppppppppppppppmmmmmmmmmmmm

mmmmmmmmmmmmppppppppppppppppppppmmmmmmmmmmmm

mmmmmmmmmmmmmppppppppppppppppppppmmmmmmmmmmm

E

m m m m m p p p p p p p p p p m m m m m

m m m m m p p p p p p p p p p m m m m m

m m m m m p p p p p p p p p p m m m m m

m m m m m p p p p p p p p p p m m m m m

mmmmmmmmmmmmmmmmmmmmmppppppppppppppppppp

m m m m m p p p p p p p p p m m m m m

m m m m m p p p p p p p p p m m m m m

m m m m m p p p p p p p p p m m m m m

m m m m m p p p p p p p p p m m m m m

Halfe Files as you were.

WHen they haue performed the former Motion, according to the direction, the Captaine commands, *Halfe Files as you were*; and then the halfe Files aduance their Pikes, and fall backe with their right legge, and so march into their proper places : and then they are againe ten deepe at six foote distance ; according to the demonstration pag. 189. Note that in turning into their places, euery one ought to turne to the right hand, which is both easier, and more pleasing to the eye, then turning to the left hand.

M M M M M P P P P P P P P P P M M M M M
M M M M M P P P P P P P P P P M M M M M
M M M M M P P P P P P P P P P M M M M M
M M M M M P P P P P P P P P P M M M M M
M M M M M P P P P P P P P P P M M M M M
M M M M M P P P P P P P P P P M M M M M
M M M M M P P P P P P P P P P M M M M M
M M M M M P P P P P P P P P P M M M M M
M M M M M P P P P P P P P P P M M M M M
M M M M M P P P P P P P P P P M M M M M

To

Halfe Files to the left hand double your Ranckes.

THis Motion differeth nothing in effect from that
before demonstrated in the 187. Figure : the
difference onely is , that here the halfe Files which
moue, march vp to the left hand of the halfe Files that
stand, whereas according to those Figures they marched
vp to the right hand of them. The Figures marked *pag.*
191. make this very plaine.

m m m m m m m m m p p p p p p p p p p p p p p p p p p m m m m m m m m m m
m m m m m m m m m m p p p p p p p p p p p p p p p p p p m m m m m m m m m m
m m m m m m m m m m p p p p p p p p p p p p p p p p p p m m m m m m m m m m
m m m m m m m m m m m p p p p p p p p p p p p p p p p p p m m m m m m m m m m
m m m m m m m m m m m m p p p p p p p p p p p p p p p p p p m m m m m m m m m m

m m m m m p p p p p p p p p p m m m m m
m m m m m p p p p p p p p p p m m m m m
m m m m m p p p p p p p p p p m m m m m
m m m m m p p p p p p p p p p m m m m m
m m m m m m m m m p p p p p p p p p p p p p p p p p p m m m m m m m m m m
m m m m m p p p p p p p p p p m m m m m
m m m m m p p p p p p p p p p m m m m m
m m m m m p p p p p p p p p p m m m m m
m m m m m p p p p p p p p p p m m m m m

Halfe Files as you were.

HAuing performed the former Motion, the Captaine commands, *Halfe Files as you were* ; and then
the Halfe Files which doubled, aduance their Pikes, and
fall backe with their right leg, to be cleare, of their Side-
men, and so march into their proper places, turning into
the same towards the left hand : which done, they will
be in the forme marked with 193.

M M M M M P P P P P P P P P M M M M M
M M M M M P P P P P P P P P P M M M M M
M M M M M P P P P P P P P P M M M M M
M M M M M P P P P P P P P P M M M M M
M M M M M P P P P P P P P P M M M M M
M M M M M P P P P P P P P P M M M M M
M M M M M P P P P P P P P P M M M M M
M M M M M P P P P P P P P P M M M M M
M M M M M P P P P P P P P P M M M M M
M M M M M P P P P P P P P P M M M M M

Cc   *Files*

Files to the Right hand Counter-march.

WHen a charge is expected in the Reare, and it being thought conuenient, to haue the Leaders of files to be in the places of the bringers vp, becaufe they are men beft able to receiue the enemie, it may be performed in this manner: The Captaine commands, *Files to the right hand Counter-march*, and then the Leaders of Files aduancing with their right legge, turne to the right hand, and march downe towards the Reare, all the body of the company mouing together ; and fo the fecond rancke, turning as the Front or Leaders of the files did, when they haue marched vp to the place where the front was ; and fo doth the third, fourth, and fift rankes, &c. The manner whereof is plainely demonftrated in the figure marked with B. and the figure marked with C. fheweth the motion performed.

B

M M M M M P P P R P P P P P P M M M M M

MMMMMMMMMM Pd Pd Pd Pd Pd Pd Pd Pd Pd Pd MMMMMMMMMMM

MMMMMMMMMM Pd Pd Pd Pd Pd Pd Pd Pd Pd Pd MMMMMMMMMMM

MMMMMMMMMM Pd Pd Pd Pd Pd Pd Pd Pd Pd Pd MMMMMMMMMMM

M M M M M P P P P P P P P P P M M M M M

M M M M M P P P P P P P P P P M M M M M

M M M M M P P P P P P P P P P M M M M M

C

ш ш ш ш ш d d d d d d d d d d ш ш ш ш ш

ш ш ш ш ш d d d d d d d d d d ш ш ш ш ш

ш ш ш ш ш d d d d d d d d d d ш ш ш ш ш

ш ш ш ш ш d d d d d d d d d d ш ш ш ш ш

ш ш ш ш ш d d d d d d d d d d ш ш ш ш ш

ш ш ш ш ш d d d d d d d d d d ш ш ш ш ш

ш ш ш ш ш d d d d d d d d d d ш ш ш ш ш

ш ш ш ш ш d d d d d d d d d d ш ш ш ш ш

ш ш ш ш ш d d d d d d d d d d ш ш ш ш ш

ш ш ш ш ш d d d d d d d d d d ш ш ш ш ш

C c 2   *Files*

Files to the left hand Counter-march.

THis Motion differeth nothing in vſe from the former; the difference of acting it is onely, that there
they aduance with the right legge, and turne to the right
hand: and here they aduance with the left legge and
turne to the left hand: The manner of doing this is demonſtrated in the next page marked with G. And the
thing done in that marked with H. And therefore needs
no further explanation.

G

```
m  m  m  m  m  p  p  p  p  p  p  p  p  p  p  m  m  m  m  m
m  m  m  m  m  p  p  p  p  p  p  p  p  p  p  m  m  m  m  m
m  m  m  m  m  p  p  p  p  p  p  p  p  p  p  m  m  m  m  m
m  m  m  m  m  p  p  p  p  p  p  p  p  p  p  m  m  m  m  m
m  m  m  m  m  p  p  p  p  p  p  p  p  p  p  m  m  m  m  m
m  m  m  m  m  p  p  p  p  p  p  p  p  p  p  m  m  m  m  m
m  m  m  m  m  p  p  p  p  p  p  p  p  p  p  m  m  m  m  m
m  m  m  m  m  p  p  p  p  p  p  p  p  p  p  m  m  m  m  m
m  m  m  m  m  p  p  p  p  p  p  p  p  p  p  m  m  m  m  m
m  m  m  m  m  p  p  p  p  p  p  p  p  p  p  m  m  m  m  m
```

H

```
W  W  W  W  W  W  d  d  d  d  d  d  d  d  d  d  W  W  W  W  W
W  W  W  W  W  W  d  d  d  d  d  d  d  d  d  d  W  W  W  W  W
W  W  W  W  W  W  d  d  d  d  d  d  d  d  d  d  W  W  W  W  W
W M W M W M W M W M d P d P d P d P d P d P d P d P  W M W M W M W M W M
W M W M W M W M W M d P d P d P d P d P d P d P d P  W M W M W M W M W M
W M W M W M W M W M d P d P d P d P d P d P d P d P  W M W M W M W M W M
W  W  W  W  W  W  d  d  d  d  d  d  d  d  d  d  W  W  W  W  W
```

The Postures of the Pike.

Handle your Pike.
Aduance your Pike.
Shoulder your Pike.
To the right hand charge.
As you were.
To the left hand charge.
As you were.
To the Front charge.
As you were.
To the Reare charge.
As you were.
Aduance your Pike.
Porte your Pike.
Comport your Pike.
Traile your Pike.
Cheeke your Pike.
Aduance your Pike.
To your funerall posture traile
  your Pike.
Recouer your Pike.
Order your Pike.

Your open order at foote.
Your close order at foote.
To the Front charge.
To the right hand charge.
To the right hand charge.
To the right hand charge.
To the right hand charge.
Order your Pike.
Aduance your Pike.
Lay downe your Pike.
Take vp your Pike.
Shoulder your Pike.
Slope your Pike.
Leuell your Pike.
Traile your Pike.
Recouer your Pike.
Charge your Pike, and aduance
  your ground.
Retreat charging.
Aduance your Pike.
Lay downe your Pike.

The Postures of the Musket.

Handle your Musket.
Lay downe your Musket.
Lay downe your bandeleers.
Hold your Rest in your left hand.
Take vp your bandeleers with
 your right hand.
Put on your bandeleers.
Take vp your Musket.
Bring your Rest to your Musket.
Open your pann.
Prime your pann.
Shut your pann.
Cast off your loose powder.
Beare ouer your Musket into
 your left hand.
Traile your Rest.
Charge your Musket.
Draw forth your skowring stick.
Short your scowring stick against
 your right side.
Ram downe your powder.
Draw forth your skowring stick.
Short your skowring sticke.
Returne your skowring sticke.
Bring forward your Musket into
 your right hand.
Recouer your Rest.

Poyse your Musket.
Bring your Rest to the right side
 of your Musket.
Beare your Rest and Musket in
 your left hand.
Draw your match.
Blow your match.
Cock your match.
Try your match.
Guard your pann.
Blow your match.
Present to the Front.
Giue fire.
Take downe your Musket.
Vncock your match.
Returne your match.
Blow your pann.
Prime your pann.
Shut your pann.
Shoulder your Musket carrying
 your Rest in your left hand.
Slope your Musket.
Vnshoulder your Musket.
Rest your Musket.
Stand to your saluting Posture.
Lay downe your Musket.

The first order of exercising Musketiers.

First vnderſtand that they are three foote in File and three foote in Rancke, hauing a diuiſion in the middeſt of ſix foote; then the Captaine bids the two firſt Ranckes, *Make ready*, and marcheth with them ſome fiue or ſix paces before the reſt of the Company, and bids the firſt Rancke *Giue fire* ; which it doth, and then marcheth away, turning to the right hand, the one halfe marching by the right hand Flancke, and the other halfe through the middeſt of the body, and ſo fall euery one into his owne File in the Reare: and then the Captaine commands the ſecond Rancke to *giue fire*, which performes all as aforeſaid ; and then two Ranckes more aduance in the former order, and ſo they may continue diſcharging with ten Ranckes a long time. The Demonſtration *pag.* 201. makes this very plaine, to which I refer you for ſpeculation. This order is of great vſe to winne ground vpon an enemie.

```
* * * *    * * * * *
M M M M M   M M M M M
        M          M
        M          M
        M          M
        M          M
        M          M
* * * * *   * * * * *
* * * * *   * * * * *
M M M M M   M M M M M
M M M M M   M M M M M
M M M M M   M M M M M
M M M M M   M M M M M
M M M M M   M M M M M
M M M M M   M M M M M
M M M M M   M M M M M
M M M M M   M M M M M
```

Dd

The second Order of Exercising Musketiers.

IN the former Demonſtration was ſhewed an Order of winning ground vpon an enemy; in this the contrary of looſing ground, or retraiting is ſhewed, and yet to offend the enemy. The diſtances and diuiſion being obſerued as in the former Figure, the Captaine in the Reare commands, *To the right hand about and giue fire*; and then the Rancke in the Reare performes the ſame, and preſently after they march into the Front, euery man into his owne File; the one halfe march on the left hand File, and the other halfe through the middeſt of the body. Then the Captaine commands againe, *To the right hand about, and giue fire*; which the Rancke then in the Reare performes, as aforeſaid, and ſo forth infinitely: all which in the Demonſtration *pag.* 203. is made plaine and eaſie.

MMMMM MMMMM
MMMMM MMMMM
MMMMM MMMMM
MMMMM MMMMM
MMMMM MMMMM
MMMMM MMMMM
MMMMM MMMMM
MMMMM MMMMM
MMMMM MMMMM
MMMMM MMMMM

D d 2

The thrid Order of exercising Musketiers.

THe whole Company being three foote diftant in Files and Ranckes (without any diuifion as afore-faid) the Captaine marching in the Front, commands, *Right Flanck to the right hand & giue fire*; & then the right hand File turneth towards the right hand, and performes the fame, and the reft of the body continues marching till they be cleare of that File which gaue fire : and then the Captaine commands againe as before ; which the then right File performes, the reft of the body marching : and fo in like manner, till all the Files haue difcharged. The order hereof is demonftrated *pag.* 205. If there be oc-cafion to difcharge on the left hand Flancke, the fame or-der is to be obferued as on the right hand Flancke. Note that when the fecond File hath difcharged, that then the firft File marcheth vp to Front with it : and both thofe with the third File when it hath difcharged, and fo forth till all front with the laft File : and then they are ready to difcharge againe, if occafion require.

M M M M M M M M M
M M M M M M M M M
M M M M M M M M M
M M M M M M M M M
M M M M M M M M M
M M M M M M M M M
M M M M M M M M M
M M M M M M M M M
M M M M M M M M M
M M M M M M M M M

Dd 3   *The*

The fourth Order of Exercifing Muskettieres.

THis fourth way in vfe, is all one with the third order; the difference is onely in the manner of performing the fame; for according to this order the depth of the Company is diuided by making the fift and fixt Ranckes fixe foote diftance each from other. The Captaine marching in the Front, commands, *Right Flancke to the right hand and giue fire,* which the right File doth ; and then halfe thereof march through the Diuifion, and the other halfe in the Reare, and fo march on the left hand of the left hand Flancke, euery man into his owne Rancke: the order whereof is plainly demonftrated in the Figure marked *pag.*207.

M M M M M M M M M
M M M M M M M M M
M M M M M M M M M
M M M M M M M M M
M M M M M M M M M

M M M M M M M M M
M M M M M M M M M
M M M M M M M M M
M M M M M M M M M
M M M M M M M M M

The

The fift Order of Exercising Muskettieres.

THis Order is another kinde of loosing ground ; the Captaine in the Front commands , *Make ready altogether*, and then saith to the first Rancke, *giue fire* : which done, the one halfe of that Rancke marcheth downe into the Reare, on the right hand of the right hand Flancke, and the other halfe through the midst of the body (which for that end is diuided) euery man falling into his owne File. Then the Captaine saith likewise to the second Rancke, *Giue fire*, which it doth , and fals into the Reare, as the first did, and so the third, fourth, fift, &c. The manner whereof is demonstrated in the Figure marked with 209. Note that here the whole body stands still, and are onely in motion by particular Ranckes, when they haue discharged, till they come againe into their proper Files in the Reare, and then stand still againe, till they haue redischarged.

```
MMMMM   MMMMM
MMMMM   MMMMM
MMMMM   MMMMM
MMMMM   MMMMM
MMMMM   MMMMM
MMMMM   MMMMM
MMMMM   MMMMM
MMMMM   MMMMM
MMMMM   MMMMM
MMMMM   MMMMM
```

Ee *The*

Clofe your Files both waies at a foote and halfe.

IF a charge of Horfe be expected, then the foote are to be in the clofeft order ; which is one foote and a halfe in Rancke, and three foote in File. The words of command for clofing Files are diuers ; as *Clofe your Files to the right hand :* or, *Clofe your Files to the left hand :* or, *Clofe your Files both waies :* the laft whereof is moft commonly vfed, and therefore I haue demonftrated that order, as you may perceiue in the Figure marked *pag.* 211.

Note alfo , that becaufe I defired to obferue the diftances precifely in all the Figures , that therefore the *Printer* was forced to change the Letters in this and fome other Figures, and in fteed of *M.* for *Muskettiere ,* hath placed *S.* for *Shot :* which I thought good to giue notice of for thy better vnderftanding.

```
PPPPPPPPPPPSSSSSSSSSS
PPPPPPPPPPPSSSSSSSSSS
PPPPPPPPPPPSSSSSSSSSS
PPPPPPPPPPP SSSSSSSSSS
PPPPPPPPPPPSSSSSSSSSS
PPPPPPPPPP SSSSSSSSSS
PPPPPPPPPP SSSSSSSSSSS
PPPPPPPPPP SSSSSSSSSS
PPPPPPPPPPP SSSSSSSSSS
PPPPPPPPPPPSSSSSSSSSS
```

Ee 2   *Clofe*

Cloſe your Ranckes at three foote.

THe Files being cloſed, at a foote and halfe demonſtrated in the Figure marked in *pag.* 211 the Captaine
then commands, *Cloſe your Ranckes at three foote* , or , *at
Swords point*; which is the cloſeſt order for Ranckes:
the which is plainly demonſtrated in the Figure marked
in *pag.* 213.

```
PPPPPPPPPPSSSSSSSSSS
PPPPPPPPPPSSSSSSSSSS
PPPPPPPPPPSSSSSSSSSS
PPPPPPPPPPSSSSSSSSSS
PPPPPPPPPPSSSSSSSSSS
PPPPPPPPPPSSSSSSSSSS
PPPPPPPPPPSSSSSSSSSS
PPPPPPPPPPSSSSSSSSSS
PPPPPPPPPPSSSSSSSSSS
PPPPPPPPPPSSSSSSSSSS
```

To the right hand, wheele.

VPon occasion of the Enemies charge on the right hand Flancke, to receiue him with the moſt able men, which are vſually in the Front; it may be performed by commanding them, *To the right hand wheele*; and then the Leader of the right hand File ſtandeth fixed, onely turning his body, and all the reſt moue vpon him as the centre: according to the Demonſtration *pag.* 215. Note that the Officers muſt be very carefull to command and ſee them to keeſe their diſtances in Rancke and File, without which, this Motion will not bee gracefully acted.

```
PPPPPPPPPPSSSSSSSSSS              *
PPPPPPPPPPSSSSSSSSSS
PPPPPPPPPPSSSSSSSSSS
PPPPPPPPPPSSSSSSSSSS
PPPPPPPPPPSSSSSSSSSS
PPPPPPPPPPSSSSSSSSSS
PPPPPPPPPPSSSSSSSSSS
PPPPPPPPPPSSSSSSSSSS
PPPPPPPPPPSSSSSSSSSS
PPPPPPPPPPSSSSSSSSSS
```

To the left hand, wheele.

THis Motion differeth from the former *pag.* 2 1 5 only
in this ; that here the Leader of the left hand File
ſtandeth fixed, as there the Leader of the right hand File
did : which by the forme of the Demonſtration marked
with A. you may eaſily vnderſtand.

THere is another way which I haue ſeene *Graue Mau-
rice* his guard to wheele, *viz.* to moue vpon the
middle of the Front, and then if they wheele to the right
hand, All to the right hand of the middle of the Front go
backwards, and the reſt forward : and if they wheele to
the left hand, then all to the left hand of the middle of
the Front goe backwards, and the reſt forwards.   All
which is moſt plainely vnderſtood by obſeruing the Demonſtration marked with B.   In which and the two former Figures is a Starre placed neere the centre, on which
the Company moues.

A

```
*
PPPPPPPPPP SSSSSSSSS S
PPPPPPPPPP SSSSSSSSSS
PPPPPPPPPP SSSSSSSSSS
PPPPPPPPPP SSSSSSSSSS
PPPPPPPPPP SSSSSSSSSS
PPPPPPPPPP SCSSSSSSS
PPPPPPPPPP SSSSSSSSSS
PPPPPPPPPP SSSSSSSSSS
PPPPPPPPPP SSSSSSSSSS
PPPPPPPPPP SSSSSSSSSS
PPPPPPPPPP SSSSSSSSSS
```

B

```
PPPPPPPPPP *
PPPPPPPPPP SSSSSSSSS
PPPPPPPPPP SSSSSSSSSS
PPPPPPPPPP SSSSSSSSSS
PPPPPPPPPP SSSSSSSSSS
PPPPPPPPPP SSSSSSSSSS
PPPPPPPPPP SSSSSSSSSS
PPPPPPPPPP SSSSSSSSSS
PPPPPPPPPP SSSSSSSSSS
PPPPPPPPPP SSSSSSSSSS
PPPPPPPPPP SSSSSSSSSS
PPPPPPPPPPSSSSSSSSSS
          SSSSSSS
```

F f

Open your Ranckes backwards.

TO open the Ranckes, vnderftand that the Front or firft Rancke ftandeth ftill, and the other nine Rancks fall backwards altogither, till the fecond Rancke be fix foote diftant from the Front, and then it ftands ftill, and the reft of the body moues till the third Rancke be fix foote diftant from the fecond Rancke, and fo till the fourth Rancke be diftant fix foote from the third, and all the reft of the Ranckes in order. The manner whereof I haue demonftrated in the Figure marked M. and the thing done in the Figure marked N.

M

PPPPPPPPPPSSSSSSSSSS

PPPPPPPPPPSSSSSSSSSS

PPPPPPPPPPSSSSSSSSSS
PPPPPPPPPPSSSSSSSSSS
PPPPPPPPPPSSSSSSSSSS
PPPPPPPPPPSSSSSSSSSS
PPPPPPPPPPSSSSSSSSSS
PPPPPPPPPPSSSSSSSSSS
PPPPPPPPPPSSSSSSSSSS
PPPPPPPPPPSSSSSSSSSS

N

PPPPPPPPPPSSSSSSSSSS

PPPPPPPPPPSSSSSSSSSS

PPPPPPPPPPSSSSSSSSSS

PPPPPPPPPPSSSSSSSSSS

PPPPPPPPPPSSSSSSSSSS

PPPPPPPPPPSSSSSSSSSS

PPPPPPPPPPSSSSSSSSSS

PPPPPPPPPPSSSSSSSSSS

PPPPPPPPPPSSSSSSSSSS

PPPPPPPPPPSSSSSSSSSS

Ff 2

Open your Files both wayes.

IN opening the Files, halfe the body moues towards the right hand, and the other halfe towards the left hand, in groffe; and then the two middle-moft Files when they are 6 foote diftant, ftand ftill, & the reft of the body continues mouing both wayes, till the next two Files are diftant fix foote from the former which ftood ftill: and fo the Motion continues in this order till all the Files haue taken their diftance of fix foote each from other. The manner whereof is demonftrated in the Figure marked with E. and the thing done in the Figure marked with F.

Thus much for the manner of exercifing footemen, fully performed, after the right order and moderne vfe of Theoricke Rules, accuftomed in thefe dayes.

Now laftly you are to lead forth your fouldiers by fiue and fiue in Rancke, in like order as is fet downe in the Figure of the order how a Company fhould march. Note that the Captaine marching out of the field, moft commonly doth march in the Reare of his Company, and his Lieutenant in the Front, the reft of the Officers are to march in like order as is demonftrated in the order of march, except you do troope out of the Field; for then you are to alter &c. howfoeuer you are to conduct the Colours to the place where they are to be laid vp, where hauing made a guard, the Captaine and his Officers repairing to the Colours, being within the faid guard, and towards the Front, he faith to the Drum or Drums, *Beat vp a difcharge,* which being done, (with fometimes a volley of fhot giuen) and the Colours wrapped and folded vp, euery man departs to his home. &c.

E

```
PPPPPPPPP  P  S  SSSSSSSSS
PPPPPPPPP  P  S  SSSSSSSSS
PPPPPPPPP  P  S  SSSSSSSSS
PPPPPPPPP  P  S  SSSSSSSSS
PPPPPPPPP  P  S  SSSSSSSSS
PPPPPPPPP  P  S  SSSSSSSSS
PPPPPPPPP  P  S  SSSSSSSSS
PPPPPPPPP  P  S  SSSSSSSSS
PPPPPPPPP  P  S  SSSSSSSSS
PPPPPPPPP  P  S  SSSSSSSSS
```

F

```
P P P P P P P P P S S S S S S S S S
P P P P P P P P P P S S S S S S S S S
P P P P P P P P P P S S S S S S S S S
P P P P P P P P P P S S S S S S S S S
P P P P P P P P P P S S S S S S S S S
P P P P P P P P P P S S S S S S S S S
P P P P P P P P P P S S S S S S S S S
P P P P P P P P P P S S S S S S S S S
P P P P P P P P P P S S S S S S S S S
P P P P P P P P P P S S S S S S S S S
```

FINIS.